Cleared for

Takeoff

50 Stories from the Pen of a Jungle Pilot

by Bob Griffin

Cover: Original oil painting by award-winning aviation artist Priscilla Messner-Patterson, Bearly Matters Studio, Sequim, WA.

Design and production by Lois Gable, Creative Touch Communications, Waxhaw, NC.

Original art (pages 13, 35, 41, 43, 47, 49, 53 and 71) by Dempster Evans, Evans Graphic Design, CA reproduced from *Beyond.*

Unless otherwise indicated, all Scripture references are from the New International Version of the Bible, copyright 1973, 1978, 1984 by International Bible Society. Verses marked LB are from The Living Bible, copyright 1971, by Tyndale House Publishers. Verses marked AMP are from The Amplified Bible, copyright 1965, by Zondervan Publishing House.

Revised edition published by Harvest Day Books, an imprint of Book Marketing Solutions, LLC, in cooperation with JAARS, Inc.

Harvest Day Books
an imprint of Book Marketing Solutions, LLC
10300 E. Leelanau Court
Traverse City, MI 49684
orders@BookMarketingSolutions.com
www.BookMarketingSolutions.com

Harvest
Day
Books

Printed in the United States of America

Griffin, Bob.

Cleared for takeoff : 50 stories from the pen of a jungle pilot / by Bob Griffin. -- 2nd ed. -- Traverse City, Mich. : Harvest Day Books, 2007.

p. ; cm.
ISBN-13: 978-1-934792-00-1
ISBN-10: 1-934792-00-4
Originally printed in 1998 by Jungle Aviation and Radio Service.

1. Missionaries. 2. Air pilots. 3. Missionary stories. I. Title.

BV2061.3 .G75 2007
266--dc22   0705

This book is available online at www.ReadingUp.com.

WHY A 50TH ANNIVERSARY EDITION?

Fifty years ago…Sunday afternoon, January 8, 1956: I was at Whiteman Airpark near Glendale, California, making final preparations to fly JAARS' first Helio Courier to Ecuador. Suddenly the electrifying news came that five American missionaries, including my friend, MAF pilot Nate Saint, were missing in hostile Auca territory. It wasn't long before I, along with the whole world, learned that all five had been speared to death on a sandbar in the Curaray River.

Life magazine carried page after page of photos of the bodies of brave men killed and thrown into the river. Nate was my friend. I was looking forward to showing him this wonderful new airplane. Now that could never happen. We all wondered, *"What good could possibly come from the senseless deaths of these five men?"*

It seemed ironic that Nate Saint's career as a jungle pilot ended in January 1956 just as mine was beginning. There was still translation work waiting to be done, and airplanes were the missionaries' lifeline to get this work accomplished. There was nothing to do but press on with a heavy heart, little suspecting that the story of this savage killing would not end there.

Nate never got to see that Helio, but among my first passengers were some of the families of the men killed by the Auca. I remember my tears and the sobbing goodbyes of their friends and colleagues when I flew Nate's family, his wife Marge, and children Kathy, Steve, and little Phillip, from Shell Mera to their new home in Quito, Ecuador's capital.

Some months later, using that same Helio I flew Nate's sister Rachel Saint and her Auca friend Dayuma, now a brand new Christian, to Arajuno, a former oil company airstrip on the edge of the jungle. A dozen years after fleeing from home in fear for her life, she was returning to her people to tell them how they too could "erase their hearts and learn to live well."

Would she be welcomed? We didn't know. The Auca remained an exceedingly violent people, killing within their tribe as readily as they killed outsiders. "George," the friendly one in the *LIFE* magazine photographs, had already been killed, speared by his own people. We stood under the wing of the Helio, held hands and prayed for Dayuma's success and safety, then watched as she hiked off into the jungle. Day after day we waited, not knowing what was happening to her. Was she still alive?

Rachel heard Dayuma first, singing her off-key version of "Jesus Loves Me." She emerged from the tangle of trees, joyfully bringing with her a gaggle of Aucas and an invitation. Admitting they had acted badly when they killed the five men, they urged Rachel and Betty (Elizabeth) Elliot, Jim's widow, to come and live in their village, Tiwaeno. They wanted to "learn to know God." They wanted "to learn how to live well."

In an act of compassion and courage which still stuns people five decades later, the women accepted the invitation. Betty, with her four-year-old daughter Valerie, and Rachel hiked in to live in the jungle with the Auca, setting the groundwork for the years of language learning and Bible translation work that lay ahead.

They relied on mission pilots and airplanes for supplies and support. There was no airstrip, and the seasonal flooding of the Curaray River had almost wiped out the remote sandbar Nate called "Palm Beach." From mid-1958 to early 1960, I, working alongside MAF pilots, flew weekly supply missions to Tiwaeno, delivering groceries and medicine by parachute. By the time I left for a new assignment, the airstrip being cut from virgin jungle was almost finished. Oh, how I wanted to land there–just once! But God had other plans for me and my family half a world away.

Now, fifty years later, the "Incident on Palm Beach" has become a modern legend. Documentaries, books and even a feature film have kept the memory of these amazing events undimmed by time. The Auca, a word meaning "savage" in the neighboring Quichua language, are now known as Waorani (sometimes spelled Waodani), meaning "the good people."

Today these good people have God's Carvings (the Bible) in their own language. They are now the evangelists, not the evangelized. They have commissioned their own missionary pilot and already have given some of their own people as martyrs.

Fifty years ago we wondered what good could possibly come from this tragedy. Now we know. The power of the gospel has "erased the hearts" of killers who now are "walking God's trails" and experiencing a peace they could never have imagined.

Bob Griffin
January 8, 2006 – Lancaster, South Carolina

DEDICATION

Affectionately, with gratitude and delight,
I dedicate this volume to
Louise,
My wife of nearly 60 years

Gentle spirit
Tenderhearted mother
Giver of herself always

Committed missionary
Companion in ministry
Coworker par excellence

And always, for these six decades,
My loving and supportive copilot.

FOREWORD

Mission pilot Bob Griffin will, in these pages, take you on an incredible journey, as you fly with him into the "green hell" of Amazonian jungle or land on impossibly tiny airstrips slashed up the side of rice-terraced mountains in the Philippines.

You will be thrilled to learn how a killer's heart was healed. "God has erased my heart," Gikita said. "Now I want to live loving the Lord." Uncle Gikita, as he is called, was one of the [then called] Auca Indians who speared to death five missionaries in Ecuador in 1956. He was solely responsible for the death of Nate Saint and helped murder Jim Elliot.

Often it's the dramatic, the heroic, the sensational that captures the worldwide press. And perhaps it should be. The news of the martyrdom of five missionaries spread quickly around the globe. Only eternity will reveal the full impact of these heroes of the faith.

But, if the writer to the Hebrews were to accept nominations for 20th century heroes for addition to his already extraordinary list, I'd like to add Bob Griffin, a missionary pilot with JAARS. He is a master with a story to tell. His story is one of serving and caring, of trust and risk. More than anything else it is a chronicle of faith and answered prayers, of victory and defeat. Woven throughout the tapestry of these chronicles is the faithfulness of God in meeting the needs of those standing alone in remote desolate places.

Bob's ministry was to be a lifeline, a channel through which supplies came. He also served as a pilot, mechanic, confidant and pastor to hundreds of grateful people. A call could come in for cement, batteries, fuel or food. Often he was airborne because of medical emergencies, sometimes in adverse weather conditions. A simple faith kept Bob on course. His servant's heart and gentle spirit are qualities to emulate.

Is God still alive? Does He care for His people? Does He answer prayer? Does He "erase the heart"? You will enjoy riding in the copilot's seat and, as you thumb through Bob's flight log you'll be blessed, as you see the footprints of God on every page.

Dr. Joe Aldrich
Portland, Oregon

INTRODUCTION

"How long did it take to write your book?" one of my friends asked. "Fifty years," I answered, tongue only partly in cheek. In a very real sense this book, now revised and expanded, has grown out of a lifetime of walking–and flying–with God, blessed by His loving guidance and wise counsel.

In actuality the manuscript had its genesis in bits and pieces over a period of several years, each chapter first seeing print in "Cleared for Takeoff," my bimonthly column for the JAARS publication *Beyond*. What you read comes from the heart of a mission pilot. My wife Louise and I are longtime members of Wycliffe Bible Translators, serving with JAARS (formerly Jungle Aviation and Radio Service).

Billy Graham, speaking of our JAARS team, once said, "These intrepid servants are quietly and carefully reaching the unreachable with the precious Word of God in some of the most remote areas of the globe." Louise and I have had the joy of being counted as two of those "intrepid servants" helping reach the unreachable for more than 40 years.

Billy knew flying on the mission field wasn't all shady and downhill. He knew that much of what we do is difficult and often dangerous. Some of what you read in this book will bear that out. I suppose that's why Billy labeled us "intrepid." But Louise and I didn't go out as missionaries intending to be intrepid. We simply wanted to do God's will no matter what the cost. In the process He let us be helpers in one of the most glorious tasks imaginable, giving people God's precious Word in their own heart language. We'd cheerfully go back and do it again if we could.

For 20 years we served abroad in Guatemala, Ecuador and the Philippines until a 1971 assignment brought us home to establish a public relations department for JAARS. Part of that assignment involved the birth of a publication. Forthwith this pilot became a writer and editor, and the epitome of the classic joke, "I couldn't even spell it, now I are one!"

While I was well versed in things aeronautical, I knew next to nothing about writing and even less about editing. But I brought the gift of a storyteller to the task, a gift I'd enjoyed using to His glory as a speaker when we were home on furloughs.

Thankfully, there were helps for a beginning writer who liked to tell stories: Christian writers workshops, books on writing, plus the tutoring of wonderfully creative and sensitive editors. They all helped teach me how to put my stories on paper so they made sense.

You have been the judges of how well we succeeded. It was rewarding to win awards of excellence from journalistic peers, but more satisfying were your warm fuzzies. Bless you for your constant words of appreciation. There's nothing more heartwarming to a writer than to have his material read and appreciated, and to learn God has used it for blessing.

Incredibly, you want more; I'm humbled and gratified. In this revised edition I've added an opening chapter and a closing chapter, plus an epilogue. I hope you enjoy all the stories from over the years collected into one volume.

Read, be blessed and give God the glory.

Bob Griffin
JAARS Center

TABLE OF CONTENTS

Why a 50th Anniversary Edition? i
Dedication iii
Foreword v
Introduction vii

MIRACLES 1
Bob, I'm So Glad You're Flying Today! 3
In the Hands of Angels 5
A Hug to End All Hugs 9
"God Has Eased My Heart" 13

ANSWERED PRAYER 15
Rice Paddies Make Terrible Airstrips 17
An Ax Head Swim? 19
Sparrows Like Me 21
Somebody Was Praying 25

PRINCIPLES TO LIVE BY 27
Bull's-eyes! 29
I Needed Help 31
Inner Strengthening 33
How Is Your Center of Gravity? 35
It's the Little Things That Count 39
Power Is Wonderful–Control Is Better 41
I'm Still Working at It, Dad 43
Let Him Breathe on Me! 45
The Storm, the Stinson and Me 47
Roosting Chickens 49
Getting Where We Want to Go 51
It Was a Barn, but It Flew 53
God's Checklist 55
Listening and Obeying 57
The Case against Sore Toes 59
I'll Never Forget the Panic 61

ATTITUDES 63

A Double Reflection of His Love 65

Mountain Men Don't Drive Airplanes 69

Real Reality 71

Eliminate the Negative 75

Hang in There and Fly! 77

Bound for Glory 79

A Time to Die 81

Through Our Father's Eyes 83

The Great Holding Pattern in the Sky 85

Where's My Shovel? 87

Don't Be a Fool 89

Getting the Right Perspective 91

Smashed Bugs, Smashed People 93

On Flying Straight and Level 95

ON BEING A SERVANT 97

What Makes You Tick? 99

Her First and Only Airplane Ride 103

Right out of the Book 107

Why Do We Do It? 109

I've Been Promoted 111

Christians Are Not Perfect, Just Forgiven 113

Move Over, Doug! 117

Just Useful Talents 119

The Big Father's Work 121

Wanted: Finishers 123

Garbage Wasn't the Word 125

Cleared For Landing. 129

MISSIONS UPDATE 135

Reflections 137

PART ONE

Miracles

Photo on previous page:

"Aviation will overcome the barrier of geographical inaccessibility."
– William Cameron Townsend in 1920

In this instance the Bible translators have only to step from the front porch to their "magic carpet" and be whisked in 20 minutes to "civilization," saving three weeks of grueling jungle travel.

Bob, I'm So Glad You're Flying Today!

It's a good feeling to look back and know that God put you in a specific place at precisely the right time for a special reason. That's happened many times in my more than 50 years as a missionary, but one incident especially stands out. It occurred one Sunday in the Philippines, and it made all the difference in a four-year-old boy's life.

In the ordinary course of events I wouldn't have been flying. We pilots guarded Sunday for a much-needed day of rest and worship, but this wasn't to be an ordinary Sunday. Late Saturday afternoon, Bible translator Ken Maryott had called from remote Balut Island asking for an emergency flight.

The saga had begun two weeks earlier when I flew the headman from a Sangir village to the hospital. Racked by malaria, the frail old man was near death, but two weeks of good care brought amazing results. Now his only ailment was the wrenching ache of homesickness, a misery that knows only one cure. He wanted to go home.

But our flight schedules for the next two weeks were jammed. To make matters worse, none of us could speak Sangir. Ken, still in the village, had to handle all the negotiations by radio. Finally, at wit's end, Saturday afternoon I radioed Ken, "There's no other way. Let's do it tomorrow, Sunday. Plan to meet us at your airstrip about eleven o'clock.

Dawn was just lighting the eastern sky the next morning when my elderly passenger and I loaded up and took off for the southern tip of Mindanao. An hour later, level at 10,000 feet, I was skimming the top of Mt. Apo, an active volcano, and the Philippines' tallest peak, when Bible translator Gordon Svelmoe burst in on the radio: "Bob, I'm so glad you're flying today. Our little Paul is terribly sick, just turned really bad this morning. Can you possibly come pick us up today?"

"Of course I'll come," I reassured him. "I should be there by mid-afternoon." Quickly we agreed where and when to meet, something not easily arranged. Gordon and Thelma Svelmoe lived in an area surrounded by terrain too rough for an airstrip. To leave the Mansaka village, they had to walk an hour to the closest road, then take a five-hour, roller-coaster bus ride that goes once a day–maybe. "The Lord protect you," I said. "We'll be praying that everything goes OK," I added, knowing that my wife on radio watch back at the center would hear and spread the word to everyone there.

Now I knew the why of this Sunday flight. In His providence, God was using Ken Maryott's problems to make me available for little Paul.

When we landed at Balut, Ken was waiting. As I helped the old man down, a big grin split his face, and he inundated me with an effusive barrage of Sangir. I didn't understand a word, but his toothless grin and a hug said it all. He was glad to be home, and he wanted me to know it. We had become good buddies.

That's one down, one to go, I thought, as I took off again. Heading my plane back north I began wondering how the Svelmoes were making out. *Did the bus run today? Will I have a long wait? Will there be enough daylight left? Well, I'll know soon enough.* I started letting down for the landing.

There wasn't a soul to be seen at the isolated airstrip, but I hadn't been there ten minutes when a rattly old car, trailing a rooster tail of dust, clattered up. This "taxi" had just *happened* to be available at the crossroads where Thelma got off the bus. Giving me a wan smile, she pushed a stray lock of hair back from her forehead. "You can't know what it means to see you here, Bob."

The memory of holding Paul, his body limp as a rag doll, while she settled herself in the cockpit still burns in my mind. *He looks bad,* I thought, and my stomach knotted in anxiety. *I hope we're in time.*

The next day Dr. Nelson told me it was close. "That boy was in the first stages of a diabetic coma. If they'd had to wait another day…I don't know…" and his voice trailed off.

It still gives me goose bumps to realize how special it was to be there: in the right place at the right time. It's not the only time God has done that for me, but maybe it was one of the best. It saved a little boy's life.

With our times in His hands, we're…cleared for takeoff, to serve.

In the Hands of Angels

Anywhere else in the mountains of the northern Philippines a big black rock, the size of a house, wouldn't get a second glance. There are lots of them everywhere.

But this particular rock, squatting malevolently right alongside the lower end of one of our down-the-side-of-the-mountain airstrips, had special significance for us missionary pilots. It was always good for an extra shot of adrenaline on every takeoff.

I have many memories of that airstrip and that big black rock, but one especially will be forever etched in my mind.

I'd gone in for a med-evac, nothing unusual at this place where there seemed to be an exceptionally high percentage of birthing difficulties. When the medical problems got beyond the self-taught abilities of our Wycliffe translator, Joanne Shetler, she radioed for help. "Bob, we've got to get Lola (or Tekla, or Yosmana or whomever) out to a doctor. Can you come quick?"

This time her emergency call came at a bad time, late in the afternoon. Normally we avoided flying in the mountains late in the day when afternoon winds often made operations treacherous. But a life, actually two, was at stake.

The approach to landing was like trying to fly down a roller coaster. I wouldn't even have tried it in any airplane other than the Helio Courier, with its marvelous controllability at low speeds. That's important when you hope to land in one piece in bad air on 600 feet of an up-the-side-of-a-mountain airstrip hardly as wide as the wings.

The patient moaned softly while we secured her on the mattress I'd thrown in the back. When she was strapped in, I was ready to go.

I stepped out in front of the airplane for a moment to get a feel for the wind and to ask the Lord for His help. While I prayed I watched, and I didn't like what I saw: a gusty, quartering tail wind bursting diagonally across the airstrip, a gale one moment, then nearly quiet the next. *That's bad news,* I thought. *I'll try to get off in one of the quiet moments.*

I took extra precautions with the pre-takeoff check. This was no time for a boo-boo. Then, with engine idling, I sat, ready to go, praying for wisdom to know the right moment, while I watched the thrashing bamboo and banana trees nearby. I waited through two or three cycles, trying for a sense of the timing.

Then it came. A calm, and I mashed the throttle full on. I wanted to get airborne quick, quick, quick!

We hadn't rolled a hundred feet when the next blast grabbed up the left wing, shook it with bulldog ferocity, and sent us crazily down the mountainside on one wheel. I slapped in full opposite control but nothing happened. That bulldog had set his teeth and wouldn't let go.

Careening down the mountain we finally bounced off in flight, but only to leave the frying pan for the fire. The wind was hurling us straight at that immense chunk of rock.

There wasn't time to react.

There was no time to pray.

It would be all over in milliseconds.

I'll never know if God made that bulldog jerk his teeth free or if a legion of angels lifted my wings, but suddenly the plane banked left, and we swooped over that killer rock with only inches to spare.

The reaction didn't set in until after I safely delivered the patient to the doctor. When I had time to think about it, I got the shakes.

It was then a verse from Psalm 91 popped into my mind, a Psalm that has been my favorite ever since I can remember. Even as a kid I was attracted to any mention of wings, and I like the imagery of finding shelter under God's wings. During my years as a jungle pilot, I just about wore out that page in my Bible. Now verses 11-12 flooded my memory: "He will command his angels concerning you, to guard you in all your ways; they will lift you up in their hands, so that you will not strike your foot against a stone."

Praise God for those powerful lifting hands! But for them, I would have stubbed a lot more than my toe.

A Hug to End All Hugs

It was late 1956, and we were on final approach to land at a tiny airstrip in the jungle of eastern Ecuador. A few minutes earlier the clearing had been swarming with happily waving Jívaro people. Now everyone had disappeared. Something had frightened them. That was bad news.

My passenger, veteran missionary Frank Drown, had asked me several weeks earlier to consider making this special flight. "But," he warned, "pray about it. It might be dangerous." Now I knew why.

We were especially wary because only a few weeks earlier five of our missionary friends had been speared to death just a few miles to the north, by people then known as Auca. The Jívaros to whom we were hoping to pay a visit were just as fierce, with a centuries-old reputation as headshrinking killers.

Frank knew that. He had been working among some of them for ten years, learning the language, making friends and developing trust. Now he was asking me to help him with a special project. He wanted to keep alive a peaceful contact his Gospel Missionary Union colleague, Roger Youderian, had initiated with a neighboring hostile group but was unable to continue. Youderian was one of the five missionaries killed by the Auca savagery.

Frank had told me that my friend, mission pilot Nate Saint, had landed only twice on Youderian's unfinished airstrip. Being asked for a difficult landing on a tricky airstrip was enough to give this green, first-term mission pilot ample cause to pray, but that wasn't the half of it. Frank said the people were so mercurial and explosive in their fear of all but intimate tribal members that he could not be sure how we would be received. He thought we would be welcomed even though he hadn't met any of them. He was known to this group only by reputation–*but a good one,* he thought– *as a friend to the Jívaros.*

What Frank didn't know was that, not long before, angry warriors from this group, intent on killing him, had lain in ambush alongside a jungle trail. Their chief, Tsantiacu, and his men were in a rage because Frank had helped save the life of one of their worst enemies. To kill was the only

Missionary planes landing on Tsantiacu's miniscule airstrip skim the roof of the chief's palm-pole house. The protective stockade around the house provides protection from attacks by deadly enemies.

response they knew. Later, when recounting the incident, they were still nonplused that on the day when Frank passed by not one of them, try as he might, could move his trigger finger. Only days before making this special flight, I had flown overhead to survey the landing area. Sure enough, the strip was a white-knuckle one, but adequate. Best of all, the people had waved a happy welcome. From our perch 200 feet above, they seemed to be giving every indication of friendliness, welcoming the gifts we dropped.

Now there wasn't anyone to wave. Everyone had disappeared.

But by now I was committed to land, so we continued the approach and touched down, still apparently without any welcoming party. Frank jumped out as we rolled to a stop. Grabbing my arm, he ordered, "You stay here, keep the engine running, be ready to leave any second." Then he started walking back down our landing path. He hadn't gone 20 paces when three men silently moved out from the jungle at the far end of the strip. In the middle was Chief Tsantiacu, waving a gun in one hand and, with the other, motioning us to go away. His warriors, brandishing their guns, added a grim emphasis as they danced threateningly three steps forward, then three back.

"I'm your friend, Panchu," Frank shouted as he advanced. That only seemed to excite them more. My stomach was churning. *I'll have to be the one, I thought, to go drag him back when he gets shot.* I was thankful for the idling engine. We could leave in a hurry if we needed to.

But we didn't need to. In a flash the mood changed. The chief, realizing Frank wasn't an enemy, quickly changed his threatening gestures to ones of welcome. Frank got a big hug, and they danced around slapping each other on the back. I shut off the engine and joined them for my hug–one I'll never forget.

Suddenly the chief changed his mood again, pushing us off and fixing us with his piercing gaze.

"Why did you shoot at us from the plane?" he demanded.

Now we knew. The engine had backfired when I throttled back to land, as it often did. I hadn't thought twice about it, but to them it meant only one thing: we were shooting at them.

Missionary Frank Drown on the right chats with Chief Tsantiacu after peaceful relations had been established. The chief, ever in fear of raiding enemies, always kept his weapon ready.

We laugh now at their mistake, but it wasn't funny then. That simple misunderstanding of our good intentions could have spoiled the entire day.

But praise God, it didn't. Six weeks later, on a subsequent visit, Chief Tsantiacu turned his life over to the One who, two millennia earlier, had called another persecutor and killer of Christians to repentance. And like that apostle, when the chief turned from being a seeker of heads to a seeker of hearts, he got a hug to end all hugs–from Jesus Himself.

"God Has Erased My Heart"

I'll never forget Gikita. Uncle Gikita, we called him, in deference to his years. He was tall for a Waorani, his deeply seamed face showing both his age and the rigors of harsh jungle life.

He would sit for hours hunkered up against one of the corner poles of our makeshift hangar in eastern Ecuador's jungle. He felt safe there with us.

There weren't many places Gikita felt safe. He had lived in fear all his life. Fear of a revenging ambush by his own people. Fear of outsiders who would kill on the slightest provocation, as they searched the jungle for oil, orchids, monkeys or other treasures. But his greatest fear was of the evil spirits he could never seem to placate.

His people were called Auca by the Quichua people, the predominate group in the area. In the Quichua language, *auca* means *savage*. But his people called themselves *Waorani*, which means *the good people*. It all depended upon which end of the spear you stood.

Gikita trusted us. He was content to sit watching as we worked on the planes, but he couldn't understand why we didn't follow his tribal law and try to revenge the killing of our friends. Gikita was one of the killers who had drawn worldwide attention some years earlier when he and four companions, wielding wickedly-barbed wooden spears, murdered five missionaries on "Palm Beach."

For Gikita, fear slowly gave way to trust when Rachel Saint and Betty Elliott went to live in his village. But change didn't come easily. He still had vivid memories of that black day when he killed Rachel's brother and my friend, MAF pilot Nate Saint, and helped kill Betty's husband, Jim.

Rachel already had a head start in the language. Some time before the five missionaries' martyrdom, she had found and begun work with a teenage Waorani girl, Dayuma, who, fearing for her life, had fled her village. After the death of the five missionaries, Dayuma, now a believer, was constrained to carry the message of God's love to her people. She returned to the village she had fled so long ago, not knowing if she would live or die. Two weeks later she came out of the jungle with a surprising invitation.

"We did wrong to kill the missionaries," her relatives had told Dayuma. "We want to learn to live well. We want to learn to know God. Tell the two white women we'll build a house for them. Tell them to come."

So change slowly started among the Waorani, and now Gikita had accepted Rachel's request to spend several weeks at Limón Cocha, our translation center, where he leaned against the hangar post when he wasn't helping Rachel with language learning and translation. During those weeks the love and acceptance he found among us began its work, but it wasn't until after he had returned to his village that he confessed the change in his heart to Rachel. "I used to hate and kill, but now the Lord has healed my heart," he told her. Gikita, the killer who didn't have enough fingers to count the people he had murdered, had learned he could start with a clean slate as far as God was concerned.

"God has erased my heart," he said. "Now I want to live loving the Lord." Finally Gikita understood why we didn't seek revenge. Gikita had become a true Waorani.

PART TWO

Answered Prayer

Photo on previous page:

The Helio Courier, capable of astonishing slow speed flight capability coupled with a fast cruising speed, quickly became the backbone of the JAARS fleet. It easily takes off and lands in 400 feet. The author took delivery of this airplane at the factory in 1955 and flew it in its first service in Ecuador.

Rice Paddies Make Terrible Airstrips

Pilots, including me, delight in bugging their non-aviator friends with corny aviation jokes. One of my favorites is to ask–with a straight face–if the hapless victim knows what the propeller on the airplane is for. Many, anxious to show off their knowledge of aerodynamics, struggle for an answer. The prop provides thrust, some say, or it drags the plane through the air. Some think the propeller makes wind over the wing to make it lift. We guffaw with delight.

"Nope, that's a good try, but that's not it. You're trying to be too technical." And then with a sly grin we lay it on them.

"The propeller is on the airplane to keep the pilot cool." When their eyebrows go up in disbelief, we pause dramatically and add, "If you don't believe it, you should see the poor pilot sweat when it stops."

It's always good for a laugh.

But there are times when it isn't funny. I'll never forget one.

I'd been hopping like a grasshopper from one tiny up-the-side-of-the-mountain airstrip to another for three or four days in the northern mountains of the Philippines, too busy to think much about the consequences of an engine failure. Anyway, it's best not to let your mind dwell on that too much. A forced landing in those mountains is something to really make the pilot sweat. There's absolutely no place to go except to crash-land up the side of some rugged slope and hope for the best.

With the project completed, I stopped by our northern translation center late one afternoon for fuel and a passenger, then headed 175 miles south to Manila, where Louise and our four daughters were waiting to begin a week's holiday. En route over a broad, beautiful valley, the engine suddenly went kachunk–a loud, scary-sounding kachunk–and smoke filled the cockpit. Almost immediately the oil pressure needle began flicking a rapid descent toward zero. I learned later that the engine's lifeblood was gushing from a horrible wound in its side and spreading an oily film all over the airplane's belly. Below, there was nothing but muddy, water-filled rice paddies. Rice paddies make terrible landing strips.

But just over the nose appeared the valley town of Cabanatuan, where some dear Filipino, bless him, had begun a small housing development. There, on the north edge of town in geometric precision, were streets all laid out and graded, but nothing else. No light poles, no electric lines, no houses, nothing but a grid of lovely places to land my sick airplane. The developer didn't know it, but he had prepared an emergency landing strip just for me, exactly where and when I needed it.

That forced landing was a no-sweat operation even without the cooling fan up front—well, almost. True, I had the security of a place to land right under me. But without power, the approach to a landing has to be just right. There is no such thing as a second chance. Goof this one up, and I'd make a muddy splash in a rice paddy. But I did it! I made a perfect landing.

Three days later, the damaged engine exchanged for one newly overhauled, I flew the airplane out, rejoicing that, even though the engine failure had put the kibosh on our family vacation, I had seen God again answer a specific prayer I had prayed for many years.

Lord, I had asked countless times, *when we inspect our aircraft, give us eyes to see the problems so we can correct them. And Lord, knowing we can't see into the bowels of the engine, please permit engine problems to occur only in such a place that we can effect a safe landing.*

Naive? I don't think so. That prayer has been answered at least a dozen times, either for me or the colleagues on my crew. I'm convinced it wasn't just happenstance that the prop didn't stop three or four days earlier when I would have really sweated with no choice but to crash-land amidst the rocks and trees on the side of some mountain. That day I learned it's not the propeller that keeps the pilot cool. It's prayer.

Cleared for takeoff—with confidence in God.

An Ax Head Swim?

The JAARS DC-3 was peacefully motoring along above the jungle in Bolivia when the right engine developed a bad case of the shakes. Without warning it abruptly vomited oil all over itself.

That's nasty news anywhere, let alone when you're flying over a jillion telephone poles camouflaged to look like trees. The crew was experienced, though. Systematically flipping switches, they shut the bummer down and single-engined to the closest airstrip, a place called Trinidad, which is nothing more than a wide spot in the jungle. No hangar. No mechanics shop. Just a grass runway and a few shacks.

The next day, stripped of its cowling, the naked engine divulged the source of the bad vibes. Five of the 16 studs holding the bottom cylinder to the engine case were broken. No major problem. Procedure simply called for replacement of all the studs and installation of a new cylinder. Experience called for such spare parts to be carried along and stowed in the aft baggage bin. Sure enough, all the necessaries were there, including basic tools.

That was the good news.

The bad news: While two of the studs came out easily, three of them, broken flush with the case, refused to budge. They seemed welded into their holes.

All day the crew struggled. Finally, tired, sweaty and frustrated, they were ready to throw in the towel. They needed more than wrenches. They needed special tools. But that was impossible in the middle of the jungle, 500 miles from the nearest help.

Lord, what do we do now, the discouraged pilot wondered as he sat resting under the shade of a nearby tree. Then he remembered an Old Testament story from his Bible reading. If God could make an iron ax head swim for Elisha, surely He could make these studs swim right out of their holes.

Foolishness? Absolutely. You don't find a section for miracles in any mechanics manual. The coefficient of friction, plus the inability to apply torque, leaves more than reasonable doubt for a swimming party of broken studs.

The crew gathered around the engine and prayed. Then, when the wrench was applied, those stubborn studs swam out. It worked! Contrary to all logic, it worked! By day's end the new cylinder was bolted in place, the engine cranked for a test, and the next day the plane was back in the air.

Yes, the prayer of faith can still make ax heads swim. Foolishness? Ask the crew of the DC-3.

Sparrows Like Me

Had I known what was ahead that crisp December morning, I might have been tempted to leave the JAARS Mooney tied down in Minneapolis and retreat to a warm bed.

Earlier, the weather briefer had served me a veritable goulash of weather. The north central U.S. was clear, but he said I could expect cloud cover over a large part of the central U.S. Not to worry, though. It was a benign system with nothing severe in it, and Springfield, Illinois, my intended fuel stop, was forecast to be above landing minimums all day. Then, after a pause, he pulled a come-along carrot from his mess of goulash and dangled it before this homesick pilot's eyes. The weather at home was gorgeous. The skies south of the Appalachians were Carolina blue.

Sounded good. A no-sweat flight, and my calculator said I should be pushing the Mooney into the hangar at the JAARS center sometime late that afternoon.

I was ready to go home. I'd been in Minneapolis for a week helping organize a committee that wanted to raise funds for another JAARS airplane: a twin-engine Aero Commander for the Philippines. They were a great bunch of people and a delight to be with, but even so I was ready for home and my own bed.

About an hour south of Minneapolis, clouds swallowed the early morning sunshine, and the instruments drew my total attention. No more sightseeing out the window. Thirty minutes later, I sat up with a start. These clouds weren't just clouds. These clouds were full of big, fat snowflakes, thousands of them, all seeming to curve simultaneously from the periphery of my vision to smack me right in the eye.

Snow? How come? The briefer hadn't served up any snow in his breakfast goulash.

It was then I heard a controller trying to help a luckless pilot find an airport somewhere in eastern Iowa.

"You're three miles out and on the runway centerline. Hold that heading. You should see it in another ninety seconds."

He didn't. The snow was too heavy.

I lost track of what happened to him. I got too involved checking out my own prospects. Springfield had gone below minimums. And not only Springfield. Every other airport in a four- or five-state area was suddenly scrubbed from the "where to go" list.

Now what? The back door was still open, but I didn't want to go back to Minneapolis if I could avoid it. The storm was moving north. Better to land as far south as possible and let it blow over. Rockford, Illinois, was still open—a good option offering friends and fellowship. I turned east, but before I had even crossed the Iowa–Illinois border, the snow shut that door.

What's happening? Where is all this stuff coming from, and so rapidly? "We missed it," the weather people apologized later.

Hoo boy, did they miss it! That storm shut down the entire central U.S. for two days.

About then the controller wanted to know my intentions.

"Simple, my brother. My intentions are to plant this Mooney on the ground someplace in one piece."

Madison, Wisconsin, some 50 miles north of Rockford, was still on the north edge of the heaviest snow. *If I can get in there, I can ride the bus back to that free bed.*

The Madison airport was like landing in Antarctica—a vast white wasteland. I couldn't see a thing. No buildings, no nothing. I wouldn't have known I had landed at an airport except for the lights edging the snow-covered runway.

"Hey, tower, I can't see anything out here. Give me some vectors to parking."

"Sure thing. Turn right on the first taxiway you see. That will lead you to the taxiway south. Turn right on it, and you should see the hangars before long."

After I parked and shut down, I sat relaxing in the cockpit for a moment, enjoying the falling snow while the gyros wound down and the cooling engine snapped and popped. *How was it,* I wondered, *that the Psalmist knew there would be times like these for pilots who had to plow through snow-filled clouds?* I don't know, but in Psalm 36, he expressed my gratitude: "Your steadfast love, O Lord, is as great as all the heavens. Your faithfulness reaches beyond the clouds"–even beyond big, fat bumptious clouds with bellies full of snow! Good to know He looks after sparrows like me.

Somebody Was Praying

One of my pilot friends has a special reason to believe in the power of prayer.

He had climbed about 1,500 feet on takeoff when the Mooney's engine stopped. It didn't gasp or cough or miss. It just stopped–as if someone had shut off the gas.

He was in a bad spot. Downtown Airport is well named–nothing but tall buildings around. No place anywhere to make an emergency landing!

A quick look over his shoulder convinced him he could never make it back to the field. It was too far away. The cardinal rule in an engine failure on takeoff flashed through his mind, "Never turn back!" He turned anyway. There was no alternative.

Pray? He'd already done that before takeoff. Now he had time for no more than an anguished *HELP! LORD! HELP!* while his hands flew all over the cockpit trying everything he knew to make the engine run. Nothing worked. Silence reigned! He was going down.

"But," he says, "the airplane glided as though Someone's hand was underneath." He began to think he might make the airport after all, at least to belly in somewhere inside the airport boundary.

Flying on that invisible support, he crossed the fence, popped the wheels down, and touched on the big white numbers on the end of the runway. Praise the Lord!

Just that day a counselor at camp and his group of kids were praying especially for JAARS pilots and God's protection for them. Imagine their excitement when they learned how specifically God had answered their prayers. Their counselor wrote, "We just want to praise the Lord and thank Him for hearing and answering our prayers."

We do too!

PART THREE

Principles to Live By

The Summer Institute of Linguistics
requests the honor of your company
at the
PRESENTATION CEREMONY
of the
Helio Courier "Spirit of San Diego"
to
His Excellency, President DIOSDADO MACAPAGAL
on Saturday, 26 September 1964 at 0930 Hours
Nichols Air Base Parade Grounds, Pasay City

R S V P
7-32-64

THE COMMANDING GENERAL,
PHILIPPINE AIR FORCE

requests the pleasure of your company at
refreshments after the presentation of
Helio Courier "Spirit of San Diego"
on Saturday, 26 September 1964
Nichols Air Base Officers Club, Pasay City

Photo on previous page:

The author with Diosdado Macapagal, president of the
Philippines, at the dedication of the Helio Courier, *Spirit of
San Diego* (CA), to the service of the Philippine tribal minorities.

Above:

Invitations to the presentation ceremony and refreshments.

Bull's-eyes!

My friend Nate Saint once said, "Landing our little missionary airplanes on jungle airstrips is like parking in the garage while driving 60 miles an hour." I've parked in a lot of those garages.

The Hohulins are Bible translators working with the Ifugao people in the mountains of the northern Philippines. Their airstrip was a jim-dandy–for them. It cut a grueling two-and-a-half-day hike to a 12-minute flight. But for the pilot it was something else. The 490-foot airstrip had been chiseled precariously into the side of a steep mountain ridge. One end was a very solid, nearly vertical basalt mountain; the other, a cliff, instantly supplied 2,000 feet of stomach-wrenching altitude on takeoff. Parking in Hohulin's garage was always an experience!

Early one morning I made three trips to get Dick and Lou and all their gear out for a linguistic workshop. After the third landing I had a few moments while I waited for Dick, so I walked back to the approach end of the strip. Like any marksman, I wanted to check the target, to see where I had touched down on each of those three "adrenaline generators."

Bull's-eyes! All three were bull's eyes! Every touchdown was within 15 feet of the others and about one airplane length from the end! I was really tickled.

Not bad, I thought, mentally patting myself on the back. And well I could. I'd have patted any pilot on the back for that. I knew it required considerable skill. It wasn't misplaced pride, just satisfaction in a job well done. I'd been practicing for a long time to acquire that skill.

All this came to mind recently when I was reading the story of David and Goliath. I have read that story since

I was a kid but had never thought much about David's skill with the sling and his confident assertion to Saul that he could do the job. I guess I'd always taken his victory for granted and assumed that God gave David especially good aim when he really needed it. Now I realize how foolish that was. As foolish as assuming God would suddenly give me good aim to spot-land the Helio Courier on a short, scary airstrip in the mountains. I'd guess that David had pegged more than a few stones at various and sundry targets!

Bull's-eyes don't just happen. David was a good marksman because he practiced.

When I was a boy on the farm, I just about wore out the .22 rifle my father gave me. I shot that gun so much I hardly ever missed. I even got good enough to toss up a little clod of dirt and leave it a puff of dust in the air. That's pretty good shooting.

I wonder if David ever tried that? Maybe not. But I'm sure he was forever plinking at all kinds of targets, moving and otherwise. Then, when it counted, David scored a bull's-eye.

"So," the Bible says matter-of-factly, "David triumphed over the Philistine with a sling and a stone" (1 Samuel 17:50 RSV).

Is that all? Just a sling and a stone, and lots of practice?

No, there was something more, something very important. David knew he couldn't clobber Goliath precisely in the forehead without God's help.

"I come against you," he told the dumbfounded giant, "in the name of the Lord Almighty..." (1 Samuel 17:45 RSV).

Goliath didn't have a chance!

Practice *and* trust–that's how to make bull's-eyes.

I Needed Help

In the 50 years I've been a pilot, it was the worst landing I've ever made. Included among those 50 are thousands of hours I've flown as a mission pilot, over some of the world's worst terrain. In all that time I've never seriously bent or broken anything. But all that changed in a fraction of a second–and turned my world upside down.

It happened on a Sunday morning after an ice storm, a freezing rain that turned our world into a slippery fairyland of glistening diamonds. I was super careful going down our icy front steps and across the driveway. I didn't have any trouble until I was on final approach, almost to the car. That's when I spun in and crashed, done in by a little icy patch of leaves.

It was bad! The crash smashed my right landing gear so badly that the doctor wondered if he would be able to weld me back together. He told me several weeks later that, for him, it was a scary break. Then he added that I could expect to be four or five months in the healing process and should be good as new within a year. Cheery thought! I'm warning you. Don't pray for patience!

Life, for me, has always been chockablock full with activity. I am the busy fellow, always reaching out to help others. I guess I have a big dose of the "gift of serving others" the apostle talks about in his letter to the Romans. And I'll always be grateful that my role as a mission pilot gave ample opportunity to exercise that gift. I enjoy helping people.

Now, ironically, the tables were turned. My crash landing put me in the hospital, and now I was the one needing help. Suddenly my world shrank to what I could reach from the hospital bed, and I quickly learned my arms weren't long enough to reach very much.

I needed help.

That's a bummer when you have always been on the giving end. Why is it that being dependent on others is humiliating? I don't know, but I do know that you must have help when what you want is two or three arms' reach away, and you have only one arm's reach to give.

Meanwhile all my buddies, members of the "Friends of Job Club," delighted in reminding me that, after all those years of risking life and limb in the mountains and jungles of the world, it only took a tiny spot of ice in our North Carolina front yard to do me in.

Seriously though, I've been so thankful during the months of recuperation that God's Holy Spirit distributed His "gift of serving others" so broadly among my friends–even to the members of the "Club." My one arm's reach was multiplied a hundredfold because God had His choice servants willing and ready to do the reaching for me. The epitome was Louise, the love of my life for 43 years, living out her vow to love and cherish.

Being made dependent became a blessing when He turned the worst landing I ever made into a beautiful experience of love. Because of all that love–and an expert welder–I was soon ready to be cleared for takeoff.

Inner Strengthening

I really expected to make the alarm ring. To tell the truth, I was looking forward to it.

Just as always at the airport, I emptied my pockets, tossing the small change, penknife and keys into a little red plastic basket. The attendant even made me give up my aluminum cane, after assurances I could manage a few steps without it.

Then, with a secret grin, I hobbled through the surveillance gate, certain the buzzers would buzz and the lights flash, even though (apart from the buckle on my belt) there was not a bit of metal on me. Well, almost none. I did possess one chunk of metal, but it was well hidden, jammed from knee to ankle down the middle of the big bone in my right leg. Dr. Lehman had used it to weld my smashed right landing gear into place. I was certain that piece of stainless steel would set off the alarm. With perverse glee I was looking forward to it.

But nothing happened.

Can you believe it? Nothing happened.

I was clean as a whistle as far as that detector was concerned. Talk about disappointment. I was shattered. There wasn't a thing to show for the trauma I'd been through. And I wanted something to show for it, even if it was nothing more than setting off the airport's security alarm.

I'm reminded of the time one of our favorite people, Joanne Shetler, was in a helicopter accident. Jo, a Bible translator in the Philippines, was along as interpreter on a flight to move building supplies into the mountains for a medical clinic for the Balangaos, the people she served. Perched happily on a pile of cement bags, she could have never imagined the horror of the next few moments.

The crash buried Jo in cement. When they dug her out she was more dead than alive, nearly suffocated, and covered head to toe in cement dust. Later, laughing but with a grimace in acknowledgement of broken bones and other injuries still healing, she said, "I'm sure I swallowed at least a bag of that cement." With a grin I said, "Never mind, Jo, it'll just stiffen your spine."

You've got to admit that's a hard way to get backbone. But then, I don't recommend breaking a leg either. There's got to be a better way to get inner strengthening and to make it visible to a watching world.

Take heart. I believe there is. There's no need to go to the hardware store for a bag of cement or an assortment of steel rods. The remedy is so simple, so easy. All we need is a daily dose of what the apostle prayed for his friends at Ephesus, "that out of his glorious, unlimited resources [God] will give you the mighty inner strengthening of his Holy Spirit" (Ephesians 3:16 LB).

That is strength impossible to hide and, what's more, we will ring true at every surveillance gate from here to eternity.

How Is Your Center of Gravity?

The little airplane probably looked a mess, considering my skill level, but in a little boy's eyes it was a thing of beauty. Now it lay, the first model I had ever built, reduced to a pile of broken balsa and crumpled tissue paper.

With a 12-year-old's excitement to see my creation fly, I had climbed the windmill to gain launching height, wound the rubber band as tightly as I dared and let it go.

Wow! It curved out and began to climb straight up. Then it bent over backwards into a loop. Oh, no! It was supposed to climb gently while the rubber band unwound, then glide to a soft landing. But not this one. It whirled around in another loop—my heart going right around with it—and then another, each time losing altitude and gaining speed. I could tell right away I had made a serious mistake. Launching from the windmill gave it more time to pick up speed. At the bottom of the last loop, going lickety-split, my little beauty slammed into the ground.

Slowly, methodically, I climbed down from my lofty perch. I had no stomach for picking up the pieces of a broken heart scattered among the wreckage. But an understanding mother's warm hugs helped mend a broken heart, and a tube of glue did wonders for the model airplane.

While mending my heart's love, I discovered that my youthful ineptness had created a problem. I hadn't made sure the center of gravity was precisely where the designer said it should be. My beautiful little biplane was horribly tail-heavy. That imbalance did it in.

It happens in real life, too. I'll never forget reading an accident report about two hapless cargo pilots whose huge airplane, for reasons unknown, was loaded with all the heavy cargo aft and the light cargo up front. On takeoff, the nose pitched up–nearly to the vertical, witnesses said. The plane stalled and slammed in, nose first, just off the end of the runway. Makes you shudder. It wasn't just balsa and tissue paper that got crumpled that day.

Balance is important. Get your airplane out of balance, and it can spoil your whole day. Getting your life out of balance brings the same result.

We pilots talk a lot about stability. An airplane, loaded correctly and properly trimmed, will fly straight and level for hours on end–hands off–no need to touch the controls. It's beautiful to see. That's stability–the end result of proper balance. I like it in airplanes, and it's something I desire in my life. Too often it seems I'm pitching nose up, then nose down, doing loops emotionally and spiritually. Uncorrected, it is certain to bring disaster.

I know. A few short months ago I slipped on some ice and did a loop or two just before I slammed into the ground. Broke my right landing gear–bad. It put me in bed for nearly three months. Gave me a lot of time to think.

My conclusion: I was as badly out of balance as that first boyhood model airplane. Year after year I've been climbing steeper and steeper at full power, seldom landing to rest and relax, not stopping often enough to refuel. It's poor operating procedure. Keep it up and airplanes will stall and crash. Humans will too.

I know. Lying abed those three months polished up my 20/20 hindsight. I believe God permitted me to slip on that spot of ice last winter and break my leg, to prevent something worse. I was at the edge of a stall, closer to disaster than I knew. Imbalance was about to do me in, an imbalance that results in something we call burnout.

Recently a word I've read hundreds of times in Psalm 23:2 jumped right off the page at me: "He *makes* me to lie down…."

Elsewhere David wrote, "You chart the path ahead of me, and tell me where to stop and rest. Every moment, you know where I am…You place your hand of blessing on my head. This is too glorious, too wonderful to believe!" (Psalm 139: 3,5-6 LB).

I believe the Lord knew I needed to slow down and rest. He knew the imbalance in my life. Since He couldn't get my attention any other way, He *made* me lie down. I'm glad. The green pastures and still waters were refreshing. He restored my soul! I could have ended up off the end of life's runway, a pile of crumpled balsa and tissue. Thank God it isn't so.

It's the Little Things That Count

A friend of mine likes clocks. He has a houseful: grandfather clocks, wall clocks, mantel clocks, clocks that show the phases of the moon, 30-day clocks, 400-day clocks, some pretty, some not so, some working, some not.

The ones that don't work are Dave Black's special challenge. Fixing them is his recreation. The pressures of business fade away while he is making an old clock look and work like new. But he says that you have to be careful with clocks–it's the little things that are important.

One day I found him in his basement, the works from a splendid, walnut-cased clock lying on the worktable. He'd just finished redoing the case, and his hand caressed the beautiful wood. "Pretty, isn't it?"

Then his attention turned to the mechanism. "Won't work," he said. "Sometimes it goes for a little while, then stops, for no apparent reason."

He got right into it. Before long he had parts scattered all over the bench–but in little dishes. Dave is a careful workman.

He couldn't find any problems in the winding mechanism, nor the bearings, nor the escapement.

Then, squinting through a jeweler's magnifier, he examined each gear with minute exactitude. "Here it is. Here's the problem. Look here, Bob, there's a tooth missing."

Screwing his jeweler's loupe into my eye, I looked where he pointed. The lack of that one tiny cog made all the difference.

I was reminded of that experience the other day when a dear friend, Carolyn Smith, phoned with mind-stunning news. Her husband, David, was gone–abruptly, unexpectedly called home to glory. Suddenly Bible translation's tick tock is skipping a beat. We don't need a magnifier to know why. Carolyn's husband would have been the last to think so, but his enthusiastic participation in Wycliffe and JAARS, including a term on the U.S. Division Board of Directors, was significant.

I don't know about you, but sometimes it takes something like this to make me realize we can't take each other for granted. We're each an important cog in God's total scheme, unique, the only one He created just like us.

Missing cogs stop the works. It's the little things that make the difference.

Power Is Wonderful–
Control Is Better

Back in the days when Eddie Rickenbacker and the Red Baron were dueling over France, aircraft engines had two power positions–full on or full off.

In fact, those old World War I rotary engines didn't have a throttle, as we know it today, only an off/on ignition switch. At contact the engine bellowed into an immediate full-throated roar. Woe to the pilot who wasn't ready for an instantaneous takeoff. That's why most of the planes we avidly watch in the old films were cleared for takeoff from the spot where they were hand-propped by luckless privates, chosen for their athletic ability and nimbleness.

After doing his derring-do over the trenches, the Red Baron, in order to get back on the ground, killed the engine by blipping the ignition with a switch on the joystick, alternately shutting the power off and letting it come back on.

I sometimes wonder if there aren't lots of people who operate like those old engines. At contact they take off to fly through life at full bore. And, in defiance of the old axiom, "What goes up must come down," it seems many don't know how to use their blipper switch to break away from combat even for an occasional landing and refueling.

Today's health experts call them Type A personalities and warn of the potential for heart attacks.

Long ago engineers discovered that to avoid catastrophic engine failure the pilot needed a means to modify the power output. Nowadays, engines give thousands of hours of dependable service because we can throttle them down from full takeoff power to cruise power once we get airborne.

I can vouch—very thankfully—for their dependable service. On my desk are several logbooks giving evidence of thousands of hours of safe flight, much of it over the most ominous jungles of the world, my life entrusted to a faithful six-cylinder Lycoming engine. It never failed me. But, I must add, I pored over—and assiduously obeyed—the operator's manual supplied by the manufacturer. I read and heeded its most important warning: "Takeoff power (i.e., full power) may be used only for a maximum of five minutes." Further, it advises the pilot to "throttle back as soon as possible after clearing takeoff obstructions." Only in dire circumstances can full take-off power be used for longer than five minutes—like when your life is at stake! Pilots are constantly reminded that disaster awaits those who disregard that warning. The engine will not run endlessly at full power.

There's another Operator's Manual, also supplied by the Manufacturer, that I must confess I have not heeded as carefully. For most of my life, I've been one of those full-bore, Type A people, always in a hurry, not giving much thought to throttling back. Now, lacking the resilience of youth, I realize I'd better be learning to use the blipper switch before parts start flying all over.

Our Operator's Manual makes it clear the Designer knew we would need a throttle, so He designed it into the system and then included clear instructions in the Manual for its use.

There's nothing complicated about it. Our Manual simply tells us to obey the Holy Spirit's instructions. He will produce self-control!

That should make it easy—and does—so long as His hand covers mine on the throttle. *Lord, let it be so!*

I'm Still Working at It, Dad

One thing I learned when I was a kid on the farm was how to plow a straight furrow. My father made sure I did.

I can still see him perched beside me on the arm of the tractor seat. I was just a little guy then, my legs barely long enough to reach the brake pedals on the old '30 Caterpillar, and my 12-year-old strength hardly enough to pull the steering levers. But I sat tall–so proud that Dad trusted me with grown-up's work.

He was an exacting teacher.

"If you want to go straight, you can't look back," he would shout over the tractor's clattering din. "Keep looking forward. That's the only way you can leave the furrow behind you straight."

Later, when I started learning to fly, I found that his advice applied in the air as well as with the plow. I can still remember Mac, my first flight instructor, short of both stature and temper, shouting over the ear-rattling noise of the yellow Piper Cub, "Pick a landmark up ahead and fly toward it. If you don't, you'll wander all over the sky. You've got to keep looking ahead."

When I became a flight instructor, I found that teaching students to fly straight and level was often more difficult than teaching them turns and climbs and descents. It takes constant attention to keep the nose from wandering off to one side or another, or up and down.

Do you, like me, find life is a lot like that, hard to keep things on an even keel, to fly straight and level, to make sure the goal is still ahead and the nose is pointed where you really want to go?

I have learned that practice with both the plow and airplane made it easier, but that's true of any acquired skill, be it playing the piano or riding a bicycle. In fact, now when I fly, it seems I can stay on course almost automatically without thinking much about it. But life–that's something different. Practice seems only to reveal that I need more practice. I find it still requires constant, careful attention to stay straight and level and not let the nose wander off on a tangent. Unhappily, I still leave some kinks in my furrow.

That's when I appreciate the memory of my father's encouragement and advice. When I'd bungle some task, he's say, "Forget it. It's done. You can't undo it. Just learn from it and try not to let it happen again." And then, like a broken record, he always finished those little sessions with the same words, "Keep focusing on the goal ahead."

Dad's advice reminds me of another fellow who plowed some crooked furrows of his own. "I'm not all I should be," the apostle Paul wrote to his friends at Philippi. "…I am bringing all my energies to bear on this one thing: Forgetting the past and looking toward what lies ahead, I strain to reach the end of the race and receive the prize for which God is calling us up to heaven because of what Christ Jesus did for us" (Philippians 3:13-14 LB).

I'm still working at it, Dad.

Let Him Breathe on Me!

"You won't notice its onset," our instructor cautioned. "And you will be euphoric; you'll think you're fine, but that's the insidious danger of hypoxia. You've got to learn the symptoms and recognize when to get on oxygen, or you're a goner."

There were ten of us, oxygen-masked like fighter jocks, and sealed up like sardines in a can. We had just spent several hours in the classroom learning the deadly danger and, more importantly, the symptoms of hypoxia (oxygen starvation) to prepare us for the finale, a simulated flight in the high-altitude chamber.

When we were all properly gussied up, our pilot was cleared for takeoff. Our steel prison never left the back room at the Shaw Air Force Base Physiological Training Unit, but by evacuating the air from our compartment, the instructor climbed us out at 3,000 feet a minute to finally level off in simulated cruise at 25,000 feet.

Then, grinning at his trapped subjects through a thick glass observation window, he ordered, "Off with your masks now, and watch for symptoms." As an ominous afterthought he added, "You'll have three to five minutes of useful consciousness."

The seconds ticked by. Nothing, just as he had said. I felt great, glad to be rid of that claustrophobic mask. But then after a few minutes I began to feel lightheaded, and no matter how hard I tried, I couldn't breathe deeply enough. An attempt to write my name produced an unintelligible scrawl. Symptoms! Another minute and I welcomed that uncomfortable oxygen mask.

Most of the others were getting their masks on too. But not Brad. He didn't seem to notice what we were doing. Ashen-faced and befuddled, he was still trying to count backward from 100 by twos. He didn't know it, but his oxygen-starved brain wasn't working right. He had gotten to the place where, without help, he couldn't have gotten his mask back on. He would have been a goner—but he still felt fine! That's sobering.

Insidious. Sneaky. Just like the instructor said.

It made me wonder how often I'm incapacitated like that spiritually. I think I'm flying high for God, doing a great job, when really I'm ready to keel over without even knowing it.

Deadly, dangerous, spiritual hypoxia–needing the breath of God in my life but not knowing it.

And symptoms? That's the hard part. They are so easy to recognize in the other fellow. But for me to see mine–that's another story.

Lord, make my "moments of useful consciousness" stretch into a lifetime of high flights for you, my life constantly bathed in the breath of Your Holy Spirit. It's only then I'm ready to be–cleared for takeoff.

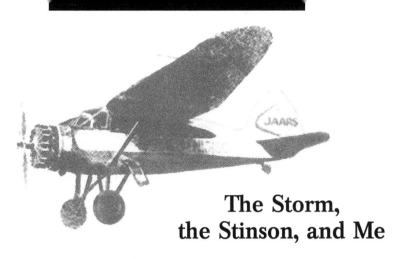

The Storm,
the Stinson, and Me

I'll never forget the day when careless directions nearly killed me.

All day I had been playing tag with the equator. My flights serving isolated mission stations had taken me all over eastern Ecuador. Sometimes I flew north of the equator, sometimes south, but always over the "green hell" of the Amazonian jungle.

Now, at day's end, I pointed the blunt nose of the venerable gull-wing Stinson southwest toward Shell Mera, a sandy airstrip whittled from the lower slopes of the Andes in the 1940s by the Dutch Shell Oil Company.

The weather ahead looked terrible—par for the course on a late afternoon in the tropics. Towering black buildups blotted out the sun and spread their tentacles into the foothills. Bucketfuls of water poured from those clouds. *Shell must be clobbered,* I thought.

"No problem, Bob. We've got lots of clouds here, but I see some blue holes here and there. It's not raining yet," radioed my weather contact in Shell Mera.

Good news. I might get through, so I plunged on. Spatters of occasional rain streaked the windshield and mingled with the old Lycoming's chin-streaking dribbles of oil.

Ah, the pimple! Up ahead I could see it, a long extinct mini-volcano thrusting 300 to 400 feet from the jungle floor. Only 30 more miles and I'll be home.

"It's raining where you're coming from now, Bob, off the east end of the airstrip, but maybe you can get in from on top. I see a blue hole or two up there yet."

I hit the wall of water just beyond the pimple. The old airplane shuddered as if we'd been pounded with a fire hose, and the cockpit turned into a shower bath. Afraid the deluge would drown the engine, I turned back and began to climb. Maybe I can get on top, find one of those blue holes he's talking about, and sneak in that way.

But climbing gobbled big chunks from the clock. At 10,000 feet the clouds still boiled up higher, and dark was breathing down my neck. A sick feeling in the pit of my stomach told me I wasn't going to make it. I couldn't waste more time probing for that shifty blue hole. I had to plant the Stinson's wheels somewhere—and soon. If I couldn't find an airstrip before it got dark, there'd be nothing to do but dump it in the trees and hope for the best.

I turned east, back toward the jungle. There was an airstrip along a river out there. Maybe I could find it before the lights went out. I tried the radio but got no contact, just buzzes and earsplitting static. *Oh, cheers! They won't even know where to start searching! Am I on the right river?* I thought so, but in the gathering darkness I couldn't be sure. *If I'm wrong, we've lost the ball game. But this old Stinson is built pretty solid. Maybe she'll protect me when we go into the trees.*

Then, there it was, barely visible in the darkness, a landing strip. Nearby, the lights of a tiny military encampment glowed through the trees. *Good! At least there's help to drag me out when I crash.* Throttling back, I lined up on the dark slash through the trees I hoped was the airstrip and groped for the ground.

The Stinson crow-hopped a time or two, its sturdy legs feeling for the surface. *I've made smoother landings—lots smoother. But who cares?* We rolled to a stop, safe on the warm breast of mother earth—and in one piece! When I tried to shut the engine down. I couldn't get my hand on the ignition switch. That switch kept dancing around all over the instrument panel.

I've never forgotten the stupidity that got me into that fix. It was bad enough to get suckered in by listening to careless directions, but worse, against gut-level instincts, I followed those directions because they were what I wanted to hear.

The apostle says "itching ears" will get you in trouble. (2 Timothy4:3).

Be careful what you listen to. It almost killed me.

Roosting Chickens

It's been a long time, but I can still hear my father admonishing my twin brother and me: "Be careful what you do. Remember, chickens always come home to roost."

He didn't know it then (he didn't become a Christian until I was half-grown) but his wisdom was a near paraphrase of the apostle's: "A man reaps what he sows" (Galatians 6:7).

I know now that Dad had a couple things uppermost in his mind. First, he was concerned for the physical safety of his two look-alikes in the midst of the livestock and around the heavy machinery we had on the farm. He knew a moment's carelessness or inattention could kill, or at least maim for life. But even more, he wanted us to guard against behavior that could blight the spirit and destroy the inner man. Now, with 20/20 hindsight, I realize how wise he was.

But what kid listens to his father? I was no exception.

My first chicken came to roost early. I was hardly five years old when I got too close to the wrong end of a mean horse. His big hoof picked me up bodily and sent me flying through the side of the barn. But

farm kids were built tough in those days. The only damage, other than the 1 x 12 board I broke on the way through the wall, was a broken left arm.

The arm is OK now, but I have a problem with another extremity. I limp on my left leg. It's not much, and normally I'm not aware of it unless someone asks why. Then I have to confess it's the result of another chicken coming home to roost. My brother and I had clambered up into the hayloft in the barn where we were struggling to move a long, heavy board. We each had an end, me backing up, when a hay hole swallowed me and I plunged about ten feet to an empty manger below. Fortunately, the cows were out to pasture so I wasn't impaled on the horns of a dilemma, but I thought I was killed. It was the first time I'd ever had the wind knocked out of me. That's a terrible feeling, but I recovered soon enough and began to howl out my hurt. The worst of it was that my left leg didn't want to work. It wasn't broken, but there was damage to the hip socket, and it was weeks before I could walk. Today I still reap the results of that moment of carelessness.

But to keep this in balance, life hasn't always been bad. I've had some good chickens come home to roost, and I'm the better for it.

Our parents saw to it that at age ten we became active in the 4-H Club, a fine organization dedicated to helping young farm kids improve their heads, hearts, hands and health. My brother and I had joint projects in poultry, pedigreed swine, milk cows and crops. The folks saw to it that if those projects were to be successful, it would be because we boys made them so. They didn't stand on top of us to make sure chores were done. Oh, there were reminders–kids need that–but no nagging. I still benefit today from the lessons of hard work and responsibility I learned. The folks made every effort to help us sow the right kind of seed. It was during those days I began learning how to use my time productively and started developing a value system that has stood me in good stead all my life.

Alexander Pope wrote, "As the twig is bent, the tree's inclined." I'm so grateful my parents cared about bending the twig the right way. Or to use the apostle's metaphor, they taught me to be careful about sowing the kind of seed that would produce a crop I'd be proud to harvest.

Thanks to concerned parents, I don't have many gimpy chickens roosting in my henhouse!

Getting Where We Want to Go

"Bob, we've got to get Marta out to the hospital. She can't deliver her baby. She'll die if we don't get her out immediately." Joanne Shetler's desperate call from the remote mountain village where she worked as a Bible translator had moved me to instant action.

But flying at 6,000 feet I couldn't see a thing except the ground directly below. Somewhere ahead were the mountains where Jo lived with the Balangao people. But I couldn't see them. I was depending on the compass to get me there.

In the northern Philippines, the farmers take advantage of the dry season to burn the trash from their mountainside plots. For weeks a dense pall of smoke smothers the mountains and valleys. Visibility often goes to almost zero. When that happens, we fly by *"pilotage"*– depending on the compass, the clock and the accuracy of our course penciled across the map.

I couldn't see. But, guided by the compass, I kept the nose pegged on the mountains I knew were there. Beyond those mountains lay the valley rimmed with rice terraces where Jo and Marta waited. If I got lost, Marta would die.

Flying in poor visibility is not unusual; it's normal. If we always had to wait for good visibility, we wouldn't get much flying done. But normal for the average pilot usually includes radio navigation aids to define route and

destination. In the mountains of the Philippines such niceties didn't exist. I had no choice but to go back to basics and depend on the compass and my watch. If I didn't I wouldn't get there. Or worse, I'd get to the wrong there.

One of the major reasons pilots lose their way is that they don't trust their instruments, especially the compass. The compass always marks the direction the airplane is pointed, but a pilot has to believe it and follow it! Pilots laugh and make bad jokes about their hapless friends who get lost. In real life it isn't funny.

I'll never forget that afternoon in the Philippines. The smoke was so thick I couldn't see a thing. But I had to fly anyway. The baby's life–and maybe the mother's, was at stake.

When I took off to get that young Balangao woman, I had two things going for me. I knew the course I'd marked on the chart was correct and I knew the compass was accurate. My only requirement was to follow it–carefully.

I did. I got to Marta–and brought her out.

It seems to me life is a lot like my flight to get Marta. The visibility is often poor. Smoke and haze obscure the way, but we have to fly. We have no choice; birth launched us on this flight. We want to make it, to arrive at the right there, because a life is at stake–ours.

But getting where we want to go doesn't have to be a big deal. We have something special going for us.

First, we can depend upon the accuracy of the course. Our Master Navigator Himself laid it out. But even better, He promised to be our guide–to let us fly alongside Him. "Fly in formation with Me, and I'll see that you get there" (John 14:6 in a pilot's paraphrase).

It can't get any better or simpler than that. There's no need to see from here to eternity when we can fly with Him. If we had to wait until we could see the end of life's journey from the beginning, we'd never take off. But we do–confidently.

It Was a Barn, but It Flew

I've been hooked on flying since I was a kid.

From the time I can remember I always had complete confidence that wings were meant to lift man to the clouds. I never doubted they could.

My twin brother and I were among those fortunate kids born in 1924, in the Golden Age of Aviation. It was the last days of barnstorming!

I'll never forget the afternoon an older cousin landed his silver-winged biplane on the hill behind our farmhouse, the wheels making narrow tracks in the fresh green wheat. He took Dad for a ride, but the day was too far spent to give rides to us, a couple of big-eyed, bib-overalled kids. Nevertheless, we were hooked. From then on the sound of an airplane passing over the farm riveted two tousled heads to the sky, mesmerized until the sound faded away.

We were 13 or 14 when it came our turn. Dad–bless his heart– somehow paid a post-Depression $15 fortune for a ride for the three of us. Mom, with perplexing logic, insisted that Dad go too, "for safety's sake." She wasn't sure those contraptions were that reliable yet.

The airplane was an immense fabric-covered barn–a Boeing 40B-4, I learned years later–designed to carry mail and up to four daring passengers.

The pilot buckled us in, and off we went, the glorious bellow of the Pratt and Whitney Wasp engine thundering in my ears and vibrating my bones. Wide-eyed, I peered out. Flight is an awesome miracle. Those big, thick wings slicing through the air were supporting us!

On what? Nothing you could see.

But that didn't dent my confidence. I had built some model airplanes and read a lot. I already knew something of the theory of flight.

And now my confidence was proved true! Me, supported on air. It was astonishing. It was marvelous. That flight gave me a sense of awe I carry to this day.

There was nothing to fear, no sensation of height, just of being suspended in space with a most magnificent view. Toy cars raced among dollhouses. And people—I couldn't even see them. The immensity of God's great world rolled out like a gigantic carpet before my spellbound gaze. How small and insignificant man's efforts seemed!

The Psalmist's question crossed my mind, "What is man that you are mindful of him?" I was stunned with teenage wonder that God would care for us, insignificant specks as we were.

Later, with Dad's help I scraped together enough money to take flying lessons. One exhilarating day the instructor shouted over the engine noise, "You'll do," and launched me solo, my Cub's fat wings drinking support from that invisible fluid we call air and feeling like extensions of my shoulders.

Suddenly I was Charles Lindbergh, Eddie Rickenbacker and "Jimmie" Doolittle all wrapped up in one. As a kid I'd about worn out our copy of Lindberg's book, *We*. Now I knew exactly what he was saying. Now I understood John Gillespie Magee, Jr.'s euphoria when he wrote: "Oh, I have slipped the surly bonds of earth, And danced the skies on laughter-silvered wings…."

From that time years ago, when I scrambled through the old Boeing's tiny door, until now, nothing has ever caused me to doubt the lift in those wings. I believed that old barn would fly. I still do.

That's how it is with God too. We've got to believe He can make us fly. When the One who wrote the laws of aerodynamics cleared us for takeoff, He promised to uphold us if we put our trust in Him—"…underneath are the everlasting arms…" (Deuteronomy 33:27).

Our confidence placed there will lift us to the clouds—forever.

God's Checklist

Years ago we simply tied a string around our finger. Today our hectic, complicated life demands more. So we make lists: grocery lists, laundry lists, "to do" lists and–for us pilots–checklists for our airplanes. All this so we won't forget what we're supposed to remember.

Forgetting an item on the grocery list may mean no cornflakes the next morning. Forgetting an item when you're flying could mean you'll never need cornflakes again.

Accident literature is filled with reports of pilots who forgot to take off the control locks before flight, or didn't check the gas, or something else equally as stupid. They simply forgot something they were supposed to remember.

Several years ago one of my buddies in the Philippines was halfway into takeoff on a short, down-the-side-of-the-mountain airstrip when he realized he had forgotten to put the flaps down. He got the plane stopped, but a lot more than his ego was bent that morning. Fortunately he wasn't hurt, but it took weeks to retrieve the airplane from its isolation in the mountains, then more weeks to make the repairs. It took even longer to unbend his ego and make repairs to his self-esteem after such a mistake.

When he finally crawled out of his black hole of discouragement, he went back to the flight line, one of our most devoted advocates of the checklist.

It's easy to make stupid errors. We all have. Some of us get a second chance. Some don't. One thing for sure: A second chance will create a fervent desire never to forget what we're supposed to remember.

But remembering: That's my problem. There are days when I wish the cornflakes were the only thing I had forgotten. Oh, I haven't made a major blunder in the cockpit. I'm too conditioned to using the checklist religiously before every takeoff. No, my mistakes come with the everyday rubbing of shoulders with my fellow pilgrims. I've let unwarranted anger boil over onto hapless family or colleagues. Or a root of bitterness eat my vitals. Or thoughts fill my mind that shouldn't be there. Or something else equally as destructive.

It's usually because I forgot what I was supposed to remember. Like "...be completely humble and gentle; be patient, bearing with one another in love" (Ephesians 4:2 NIV).

Or, "...be careful how you act.... Don't be fools; be wise: make the most of every opportunity you have for doing good" (Ephesians 5:15-16 LB).

Those *and more* are all on God's checklist. We won't forget what we're supposed to remember if we'll just use it.

Listening and Obeying

Lots of flying stories begin: "I'll never forget the time I was at 10,000 feet…"

But really, I won't!

I was at 10,000 feet in thick clouds on my way to Minneapolis on an instrument flight clearance when…but let me back up.

Before takeoff on an instrument flight the pilot must have a clearance. That's the pilot's flight plan, approved, put in the computer and issued by the air traffic controller, to confirm that everybody in the system knows and understands just what the pilot plans to do. Once the pilot accepts his clearance, he must obey it, ask for an amendment, or cancel.

Now, back to 10,000 feet on my way to Minneapolis. About 120 miles before my planned arrival, the controller gave me an amended clearance to a different arrival airway, for reasons of traffic flow. Ten or fifteen minutes later I made what could have been a fatal error. When I crossed the navigation fix identifying the new route, I totally forgot to change to the new clearance and proceeded blithely up the wrong airway—the one I'd originally requested. For 20 miles or so I followed the wrong track before the controller (watching my boo-boo on his radar screen) asked my heading (his genteel way of asking where I was going and why).

Suddenly I came to! I was going the wrong way on a one-way street! I hadn't obeyed my clearance. It could have been a fatal mistake. But the controller was watching and directed me out of danger.

I find my life as a Christian is a lot like that. The Lord will keep me on track in clear airspace if I listen and obey his instructions.

One of God's earlier fliers affirmed it when he told the whole world:

> You chart the path ahead of me, and tell me where to stop and rest. Every moment, you know where I am. You know what I am going to say before I even say it. You both precede and follow me, and place your hand of blessing on my head. This is too glorious, too wonderful to believe! (Psalm 139:3-6 LB).

I'm in the Psalmist's camp. Years ago when I filed my flight plan with the Master Controller, He gave me a clearance to my requested destination with the route spelled out and a map and all the navigational fixes I need. That was God's promise and provision when He cleared me for takeoff!

But once in the air, I have a responsibility to fly right. If I reject His plan for my life and His control, I'll crash. He will vector me around the thunderstorms, make sure I miss the mountains and bring me out on course and right-side up, as long as I'm willing to follow His instructions. The consequences of anything less are too terrible to contemplate.

I'm cleared for takeoff—under His control.

The Case against Sore Toes

Trying to weasel out of blame is a problem as old as Adam.

"The woman you put here with me, she made me do it."

What a guy, blaming his wife! But Eve had a ready response: "The serpent tricked me."

Already the problem is endemic. But before you judge your ancestors too harshly, consider how long it has been since you tried to shift the responsibility for a mistake to someone or something else. We're often as quick as Adam and Eve to offer lame excuses and, frequently, as irrational about where we lay the blame.

It reminds me of the little boy my mother told about. (No, it wasn't her little boy!)

As a young bride, and still missing the schoolroom and the students she left behind to become a farmer's wife, Mom enjoyed the occasional visits of a neighbor's ten-year-old boy. Sid would ride his old white mare bareback the mile or so from his house and tie her to the plow in the barnyard while he had cookies, fresh milk and conversation with Mom.

When it was time to go, Sid faced a major problem. He was too short to get on the old mare.

His solution was simple. With his shoulder in the mare's belly, he pushed her up close to the plow. That would be his launching pad.

But the mare was wise to the ways of a boy too short to mount normally. When Sid was all set to jump after climbing up on the plow beam, she sidled away to stand just out of reach. If old white mares grin, she must have had a big one.

Not Sid. He was enraged. But to give him credit, he was tenacious. It wasn't until after the third jump at a target that kept moving out of reach that Sid's safety valve popped. He picked himself up out of the dust, squared off, and kicked–the plow.

Stupid? For sure! But not a lot more, it seems to me, than Adam's swipe at Eve. Or hers at the serpent. And us? If we're honest, we'll all admit to our own bloodied toes.

But the problem is much more serious than sore toes. A young Psalm singer learned that lesson. In cadences familiar to many of us, David chronicles the lessons he learned from hard experience.

"There was a time when I wouldn't admit what a sinner I was," he writes, "but my dishonesty made me miserable...my strength evaporated...until I finally admitted all my sins to you and stopped trying to hide them. I said to myself, 'I will confess them to the Lord.' And you forgave me! All my guilt is gone" (Psalm 32:3-5 LB).

Just a few words, but in them, David says it all. No need to kick the plow or even the horse!

That's how to unload the blame—and the burden.

I'll Never Forget the Panic

Panic choked my throat when I realized I was lost. The flight I was so sure would be a piece of cake had turned into a can of worms.

I was 19, a green 70-hour pilot, ferrying a two-seater Luscombe airplane more than halfway across the U.S. I had jumped at the offer to make the first really long, cross-country flight of my new career, from Minnesota to Washington State. *WOW*, I thought, *what fun! A first-rate learning experience along with adventure.* I didn't know the half of it!

Early on, the flight went well. But it didn't last. I got lost–and scared. Panic, I learned, quickly destroyed my ability to think clearly. At the moment I knew only two things for sure: I was scared, and I was somewhere in the middle of South Dakota. But where? Nothing on the map matched anything on the ground. In my panic I began to wonder if north was north and south was south.

The pilot's old joke, "You're never really lost until you run out of gas," was suddenly a lot funnier in the airport coffee shop than here in the cold confines of my noisy cockpit. I was so discombobulated, I hardly knew which way was up.

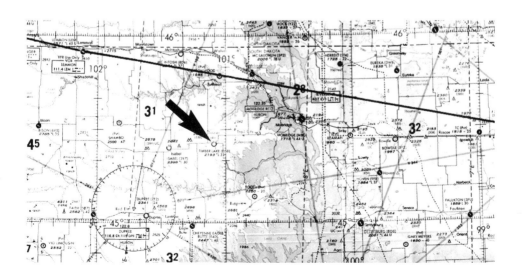

And worst of all, I had been so certain I knew my location. Since early morning, between refueling stops, my finger had carefully followed the plotted pencil line marking the route on the map. Until now everything had gone well. Towns came up on cue. Rivers were where they belonged and roads ran in the right direction.

Now the whole world had gone crazy. I wondered if I could believe the compass. It surely couldn't be right.

But it was right–and now I hang my head in shame to think how dumb and disbelieving I was. But I was so sure I knew where I was until…

I'm reminded of a comment the man known as the Bible's wisest man made about navigation and steering the right course. In one of his proverbs he said, "You may think you know the way to the airport, but you won't find it. Your way leads to death" (Proverbs 14:12 in a pilot's paraphrase).

I know Solomon wasn't speaking of my next fuel stop, but he had my interest at heart. My bones might still be bleaching on the plains, if I hadn't found the way.

My mounting panic turned to relief when I chanced upon a blacktopped road, followed it to a town, and read the name on the water tower. (Bless you folks in Timber Lake for being proud enough to emblazon the name of your town for lost pilots to see.)

Suddenly everything fell into place. The roads ran east and west again, as the map said they should, not south as my head said. And amazingly, even the compass swung around and pointed the right direction.

I knew the way!

Lord, thank you for the water towers you put in my path, and your compass, which always points the right way.

PART FOUR

Attitudes

Photo on previous page:

A happy but curious throng welcomes author Griffin and translator Betty Elkins to a remote village deep in the jungle of Mindanao, Philippines. The airplane quickly converted a difficult, dangerous, five-day overland trip into an easy, comfortable half-hour flight.

A Double Reflection of His Love

For most of my life I've never needed a mirror to see what I looked like. I just looked at my brother.

We had the same cowlicks, same mannerisms, even the same cavities in our teeth. The first four or five years, Mom and Dad couldn't tell us apart at a distance. We got called Buddy a lot. Mom dressed us in identical outfits all through school. Even when we were in college we never bought just one of anything. We enjoyed being each other other's reflection.

It made for some fun times. I remember when our fourth grade classmates egged us into changing seats when our teacher had to leave the room for a few minutes. We could have pulled it off except for the tittering excitement that filled the room on her return. I suppose, too, that we both looked a bit guilty.

We did, however, achieve one coup I'll never forget. During World War II my brother had a week's leave from the navy. He came home to the family farm, which I was managing thanks to the local draft board's decree. On Friday night we attended a meeting of the InterVarsity Christian Fellowship on the nearby campus of Washington State College.

He wore my civvies. I wore his uniform. We traded girlfriends, and no one knew it for the entire evening. Making it up to the girlfriends later wasn't all that bad either.

One of our favorite local merchants always seemed to know who was who. It took me years to understand his simple stratagem.

"Hi," he'd call out when we went into his shop. "How's Robert?"

"Oh, I'm fine, Ernie," I would answer, or if it was my brother answering, he'd say, "He's OK." It always worked.

We fooled lots of people, but I've never been able to fool my wife. It wasn't for lack of trying. When we were dating, I picked her up at her college dorm to come to supper at the farm. My brother was home on leave again, and this would be her first opportunity to meet him. For camouflage I wore one of his gob hats and one of his navy denim shirts with the sleeves rolled up. A toot on the horn of our four-ton, orange, Dodge truck brought her running to the curb.

"Hi, you must be Louise. I'm Richard. Robert is busy, and he asked me to come pick you up. Boy, you're just as pretty as he said you'd be."

Her green Irish eyes looked me up and down while thoughts of my earlier brags about fooling people circled around behind those pretty eyes. Then her freckles crinkled with a grin. "Ha, you can't fool me. What about that brown spot on your arm?"

Those rolled-up sleeves and a little brown birthmark on my left arm did me in.

In 1960, when we came home on furlough from our missionary work in the jungles of Ecuador, my brother asked me to tell his high school biology class about the flora and fauna of the rain forest. It delighted him to introduce his twin brother. Ever the teacher, he spent a few minutes telling the class something about the physiology of twins, identical and fraternal.

Then, turning to me, he urged, "Be sure to tell them why you go to the jungle and what you do there."

His missionary passion for his kids was a reflection of mine. During my lecture a messenger came from the office. Seeing me in the front of the class, she stepped in with a note. My brother, standing in the corner out of sight, stepped forward to meet her. She looked at him, then looked at me, went white, gasped, and fled, a blast of delighted laughter chasing her down the hall.

We had our fun, lots of it down through the years. But the strongest and most lasting memories are not of the laughs we had fooling our friends. The best memories are of the joy we had in reflecting not just each other, but God's love.

I was especially proud when I saw the results in some of his students with special needs, who found they could bask in the love of a teacher who cared. I knew his concern spilled from a heart filled to overflowing by the Lord who, in answer to a mother's prayers, had called each of us to mirror

His love—me to the Bibleless people groups, Richard to godless high school students.

We can't reflect each other anymore. Half of me is gone. Cancer took my brother home to glory in December 1987. But my loss is his gain. And, as the apostle expressed it, he has the better of it.

And me? All I can do is keep on keeping on, working toward that day when I shall finally be all that Christ wants me to be, a mirror that brightly reflects the glory of the Lord.

That's the reflection that will really count.

Mountain Men Don't Drive Airplanes

Ama Canao says I taught him to fly. Well, I did–sort of.

I wish you could have been there that summery day in the Philippines when Ama climbed out of the Helio Courier after our flight. He was feeling ten feet tall, so excited he could hardly talk. And proud–it's not every day a mountain man, not long out of the spear-and-ax culture, has the opportunity to drive an airplane.

It all started when Joanne Shetler, Wycliffe translator working with the Balangao people, asked me to fly to Botac, a cluster of houses clinging to the mountainside, and pick up Ama. He had agreed to leave his rice-terraced mountain valley for two weeks to help Jo in a linguistic workshop.

As I flew to the mountains, I reflected on this man we all called Ama. The word *ama* (meaning father, grandfather, or revered one) is a universal title of respect in the Philippines. I always used it for Ama Canao, not only out of respect, but even more because I had come to dearly love this wiry, capable man. Jo and her translation co-worker, Anne Fetzer, also called him Ama, but they did it because he was literally their father in the village. He adopted the girls into his family and helped and protected them as he would blood kin. He was a key ingredient in their Bible translation ministry.

Ama had learned many skills in a lifetime of surviving under difficult circumstances, but there was nothing in his background that applied to flying. However, he was mentally keen, physically quick, and always eager to learn new things.

As he hitched up his pants and grabbed a handhold to swing himself into the cockpit, I impulsively asked, "Did you ever drive an airplane, Ama?"

"Oh no, Mr. Bob," came the quick reply, but his eyes sparkled with the idea.

"Maybe you'd like to try," I suggested, patting the copilot's control wheel beside me.

Hesitantly, he reached out to touch the wheel, then burst out, "Oh yes, Mr. Bob!" as a grin that threatened the security of his new dentures split his face.

Our roller-coaster takeoff down the mountainside didn't bother him at all. He'd already flown with JAARS pilots many times. But he had never handled the controls. Gingerly, he experimented under my instructions. Sure enough, just as I'd told him, turning the wheel to the right dropped the right wing, and we turned to the right. Pulling back on the wheel made us go up; a push forward and we went down. He turned us first one way, then another, his eyes dancing with delight. The airplane obeyed his every command. Ama could fly!

I pointed out the saddle-backed ridge bulking up from the valley's floor some thirty miles away. "That's where we're going, Ama. You drive us over there." He did, and made a pretty good job of it too.

Two weeks later when he went home–he drove on that flight too–he proudly told everyone how Mr. Bob taught him to fly the plane. But his excitement fell on deaf ears. He was dumbfounded to find no one believed him, not even his wife Ina. "You lie. Mountain men don't drive airplanes," she huffed, summarily dismissing his wild tale.

I guess we all have a problem understanding and believing something out of the ordinary. I'm sure Moses, his ears ringing with Israel's complaints, could empathize with Ama. Probably Peter too, remembering a servant girl who answered his unexpected knock at the door. In fact, I seem to remember another fellow saying, "Except I see the print of the nails in his hands…" (John 20:25 KJV).

Real Reality

I was still settling in, buckling my seat belt, when Dave began explaining the intricacies of getting the "Big Ugly Fat Fellow" off the ground.

"I'll manage the throttles for you, Bob. You'll be busy enough at first just flying the airplane," Dave told me.

I guess so, I thought, as I fingered the biggest "fistful o' throttles" in the U.S. Air Force–eight of them–and curled my hands around the massive control wheel. I'd never tried to fly anything so big before. The crews affectionately call their airplane *BUFF,* short for Big Ugly Fat Fellow. I didn't think the B-52 so ugly or fat, but it sure was big.

We rumbled down the runway forever, it seemed, acceleration much slower than I'd anticipated from those eight big engines.

"Hold the control yoke in your lap, all the way back. The nose will come up of its own accord when she's ready to fly. Then when we're airborne, go well forward with the control, or she'll pitch up into a stall," Dave warned.

In my mind's eye I saw trails of black jet smoke streaming behind as we thundered into the air. "Level off and stay in the pattern," Dave ordered. "We'll come around and do some landings."

Holding the speed down to 150, I wrestled the monster around. The B-52's wingspan was longer than some of the jungle airstrips where I've landed, and the *BUFF's* 4,000 square feet of wing area was twice the area of the average middle-sized house. Sitting on the front porch and flying a house takes muscle.

The approach path I flew returning to the runway would have made a snake dizzy. I was struggling to learn how much and when to muscle the controls. The landing was anticlimactic, but a good one! Dave put the power to it, and we did two more. By the time we came around the third time, I'd straightened out my snake-trail approach enough that Dave could say, "Not bad, Bob. Not bad. Now lets go get some fuel. Take us up to 15,000 feet."

The tanker was there, waiting. "Control your airspeed to match the tanker; now slide underneath–easy does it–to hook up to the fueling boom." Then Dave took the controls. "See how I'm lining up those three lights on the tanker's belly? You can't miss. Kachunk. Dave had a connect.

Then he let me try. I did it! I hooked up. Twice. My grin must have gone from ear to ear.

"Not bad, Bob," Dave grinned in response. "It's seldom first timers get a connect. You got two. Now head west toward the mountains and take us down to about 400 feet. We'll do some low altitude work."

At 400 knots, it wasn't long before the lower slopes of the Rockies' Wind River Range filled the windscreen. "Fly down the valleys but clear the ridges by at least 100 feet," Dave ordered.

Wow, this was flying! I hadn't had so much fun since I was a teenager. It reminded me of the times my buddy and I dodged among the wheat-covered hills of eastern Washington, playing tag in our J-3 Cubs.

But all good things come to an end. "Time to take us home," Dave said, and I reluctantly climbed for altitude and pointed us east. I greased on the last landing and held that big beaut straight down the runway while our speed bled away.

Then Dave did a strange thing. Instead of directing me to taxi to the ramp, he reached up and flipped off the switches. Suddenly the windshield went blank. The runway was gone. There was nothing there, no airport, no taxiway, no nothing.

Dave and I had just been up in the *BUFF* flight simulator at a Strategic Air Command base. Our flight was all sham–simulated–a fantastic, multimillion-dollar trick to make me think I was flying when we hadn't moved a foot.

I think much of what we call Christianity today is like that. We sit in our multimillion-dollar sanctuaries, go through all the motions and procedures and think we're really flying–but it's all sham. There's no reality. We never get off the ground.

I think if Jesus were here today, He might use flight simulators to make a point about the lack of reality in our frantic, activity-filled lives. He had some hard words for a similar situation: "You hypocrites!" He told the Pharisees. "Well did Isaiah prophesy of you, 'These people say they honor me, but their hearts are far away. Their worship is worthless…' " (Matthew 15:8-9 LB).

It will be awful to have to say, when the windshield goes blank, "But, Lord, it seemed so real."

Eliminate the Negative

When William Cameron Townsend, a slender, unpretentious 21-year-old, first arrived in Central America to give missionary life a try, the welcoming committee wasn't very impressed. Behind his back one said, "That skinny Townsend won't last two months."

That was a masterpiece of poor judgment. Proving to be durable, Townsend, the founder of Wycliffe Bible Translators, lasted 85 productive years!

All his life Townsend accentuated the positive. The words *not* and *no* were not a part of his working vocabulary. He expressed his philosophy best in this poem he wrote as an underweight college freshman with a schoolboy-like wish for a ball player's physique:

LIMITATION

Oh, hateful word
That halts your aspirations,
That downs your dreams
And brands your schemes
As filmy speculation
And says, "You shan't
Because you can't"
In the face of limitation.

Deceptive word
That means procrastination;

That bids content
With every stint,
And pillows lowly station,
And says, "Just wait
Till time and fate
O'ercome your limitation."

Yes!
The challenge word
That dares against stagnation,
Brings out your stuff
And frightens bluff
With every consternation,
And calls for might
And bids you fight
To climb o'er limitation.

Am I bold enough to do the same?

Hang in There and Fly!

As a pilot I've flown in my share of poor weather. To be honest, if I had my druthers, I'd always fly in the sunshine. Who wouldn't? But experience tells me there will be days with nothing but clouds. And rain. And misery.

Years ago Annie Johnson Flint wrote a short poem. You may know it–or parts of it. The first line is the one that pops up in my memory, especially when I'm bouncing along in stormy weather with rain sluicing off the windshield. It goes like this:

> God hath not promised skies always blue,
>
> Flower strewn pathways, all our lives through…

I think maybe Annie Johnson Flint had flown in a cloud or two!

I wonder if there were times when she wanted to ask God to stop the world and let her off. I've been ready for that a time or two, but I learned long ago you can't quit just because the flight is tough.

I'll never forget my demanding instructor during instrument training. Because of his schedule as an airline pilot, he had to give me training in big gulps instead of the preferred regular small daily bites. Sometimes after four or five hours of continuous intense training, I'd be so tired and mentally discombobulated I was ready to throw up my hands and give up. I wanted to quit.

"Hang in there and fly," he'd demand. "You're not done until you shut the engine down on the ramp. Come on! Fly the airplane!" Then, to prove to him I could, I'd grit my teeth and keep on keeping on.

Many times since then I've been grateful for the discipline he instilled in me in those days, because along the way I've had my share of cloud. And rain. And misery.

Oh, there have been some wonderful sun-filled days too, when I reveled in the joy of the task. But there were times I wanted off–or out–or just to disappear.

I'm certain Annie Johnson Flint enjoyed the sunshine but also had known her share of cloud. And rain. And misery. But she had learned–as we all must if we're going to keep the airplane of our life right side up and on course–that the ultimate source of strength is not in our skill or personal discipline, as important as that is. So Annie Johnson Flint concluded her poem with this affirmation:

> …God hath promised strength for the day,
> Rest for the labor, light for the way,
> Grace for the trials, help from above,
> Unfailing sympathy, undying love.

Bound for Glory

"Are you a first-class passenger?" the stewardess asked one of my JAARS buddies as he boarded the airliner.

"Yes, ma'am," he said with a disarming, lop-sided grin. "I sure am."

"But," she said, frowning at his ticket stub, "it says here that you're in the economy section."

"That's right," he quipped. "I'm flying economy today, but I am a first-class passenger."

The stewardess was as quick as he. "Yes, sir," she said, looking up with a big smile. "On this airline, no matter where they sit, everyone is a first-class passenger. Welcome aboard."

We may grin at my buddy's tomfoolery, but, for all his jesting, he made a point, and the stewardess was quick to affirm it. Each of us wants to be recognized as a first-class passenger in the airliner of life, no matter where we sit.

On a recent trip I had to check into a motel for the night. On the wall in the lobby, emblazoned in big gold letters, was the message, "You're Somebody Special."

They really didn't have to tell me. I knew that already. But I was glad they recognized it. I was lonesome and tired–three weeks into a grueling six-week speaking tour–and very much in the mood to be treated as someone special, a first-class customer, no matter what room I slept in.

That evening, enjoying the comfort of their good bed after a soak in the Jacuzzi, I reflected on the aptness of their motto. The manager was canny enough to know that every customer wants to be special, that everyone wants first-class treatment.

Some time ago my wife and I watched a rerun of an old Lawrence Welk, all-Gershwin program, all the old favorites. One number particularly struck me. You remember it, I'm sure: "Somebody loves me, I wonder who. I wonder who it can be."

Gershwin penned a beautiful melody, one that's easy to hum. But the lyrics are so terribly sad, filled with sorrowful longing.

I've thought of those words numerous times when the tune–it's the kind that sticks in your memory–pops up unbidden.

Many people go through life figuratively singing that song, desperately looking for someone to love them, someone who will say, "You're special to me."

Thinking about that song's pensive message makes me appreciate even more how blessed I am. With certainty I know somebody loves me, that I'm special to a lot of people–family and friends. But what really boggles my mind is to realize how special I am to God–so special that He chose me to be His own even before He made the world (Ephesians 1:4).

I don't understand it. But I don't have to, any more than I have to understand the wholehearted love my wife and four daughters have for me. I just accept and revel in it.

How blessed I am! Somebody loves me. I don't have to wonder who. And, best of all, because of my Lord's special love for me, I'm booked as a first-class passenger on a flight bound for glory.

A Time to Die

Darlene Bee was an extraordinary person: Bible translator, Ph.D. in linguistics, educator, scholar, thinker, teacher in courage and sensitive friend. But she was more than just a creative mind. The Usarufa people of Papua New Guinea among whom she worked called her the "carpenter girl." She taught them how to use tools.

She was a rare combination of practicality, science and artistry with language, her chief medium. It was to paper that she committed some of her deepest thoughts in beautiful poetry.

In April 1972 Darlene was suddenly "cleared for takeoff" to a higher realm. She and six others were killed in a tragic plane crash near Lae, Papua New Guinea. By a miracle, her briefcase was the only piece of luggage to survive the crash. Among her papers we found this poem:

A TIME FOR DYING
(Ecclesiastes 3:2)

Perhaps the moment after ecstasy;
after feeling the full fierce force of life;
after knowing love
and while love is still warm
Perhaps that is the time for dying;

before everything and one
has turned sour;
before life is a burden,
before the thrill of waking
to a new day is gone;

before we long for death…
to die while bursting with life,
brimming with vitality,
longing to live–

Perhaps this is the time
to die and live.*

That's the takeoff clearance I always want to be ready for.

*Chenowith, Vida. 1973. From *Bravo, Lord!* Used by permission.

Through Our Father's Eyes

Webster defines perspective as "the capacity to view things in their true relation." We might say, in everyday speech, it's the ability to see things as they really are.

One of my passengers in Ecuador had a problem with that. Bill, sitting in the copilot's seat beside me, was a graduate civil engineer, new to the jungle and to his untried life as a Bible translator.

We were landing at a jungle airstrip that appeared from a distance to be a mere machete slash in the midst of the trees. I knew Bill was getting more tense as we got closer. But, concentrating on the tricky landing, I didn't think much about it. A newcomer normally got an extra shot of adrenaline landing in such a place–even I did.

But I never expected Bill's reaction. He jabbed his elbow in my ribs and in pure panic shouted, "Pull up, Bob. Pull up! It'll never fit!"

He was certain we were about to crash. His engineer-trained eye knew the outstretched wings of the Helio Courier would never fit between the giant jungle trees.

But the Helio did fit. I knew it would. I had been there before. I had a different perspective.

Just the other day we couldn't understand why a ferry flight, carefully planned and prepared, was delayed. From our perspective we knew the Cessna 206 was ready to go–safely–all the way across the Atlantic to Liberia. But it had an irritating, miniscule fuel leak. Safety was not jeopardized. The flight could have gone, but our JAARS mechanics were hesitant to release the airplane. Something told them they had to fix that leak, minor as it was. Theirs was a different perspective–a God-inspired perspective, as it turned out.

The mechanics worked for three days trying to repair the leak. Before they found the problem a message from a trusted parts supplier arrived: "You may have faulty engine valves. Check it out."

You can guess the rest. It was only then we knew–with new perspective–that God had delayed the flight for a reason. We're thankful for mechanics sensitive to God's still, small voice. They knew what they had to do.

There are some things we'll never see except through God's eyes. That's the only way we'll have the ability to see things as they really are.

The Great Holding Pattern in the Sky

I get impatient when I have to hold. It drives my frustration level way up, no matter whether the instructions come from a telephone operator or from an air traffic controller. Even the soothing music some companies play to fill the idle waiting minutes doesn't do much but keep my fidgety fingers on the beat. And Air Traffic Control doesn't even play music!

Centuries ago God put His elect people into a hold–a long hold–an "until this generation passes away" hold. For three decades the Israelites beat the Negev sand to dust, going around and around and around.

Their hold was a result of disobedience. They goofed. Badly. They missed His command. They failed to trust Him.

But not every hold is the result of disobedience or lack of faith. It may be that God just has to get us into sync with the rest of the traffic.

I'll never forget the traffic controller's instructions one time on a flight from Waxhaw to Dallas: "Hold southeast of Scurry, maintain 10,000 feet, expect further clearance at 43 past the hour." After three and a half hours of flying on instruments, we had, just minutes before, broken out of the storm clouds into gorgeous, relaxing sunshine. In the clear air we could almost see our destination. I couldn't believe the controller was making us hold.

We weren't alone. Stacked above us were two airliners, Delta 1105 and Eastern 799, orbiting the same invisible racetrack in the sky, waiting like us for clearance to proceed.

Flying around in an aerial merry-go-round with our destination, Red Bird Airport, almost in sight was frustrating. Holds are to be expected when the weather is really lousy and the controller has to get everybody properly sequenced for instrument landings, but on a beautiful, clear afternoon with hardly a cloud in the sky, it didn't make sense.

I was tempted to cancel my instrument flight plan, but I had to assume the controller knew something I didn't. On his scope he saw all the planes I couldn't see. So I hung in there, going around and around. It was only ten minutes until clearance came to proceed, but it seemed like forever. To this day I don't know why he had us in a holding pattern, but I obeyed by faith.

There are times God puts us in a holding pattern, and we're impatiently tempted to cancel His option on our lives and head off without His control. Israel may have beat the Negev to dust, but at least they did it in God's presence (a cloud by day and fire by night). Had they left that Sinai holding pattern without God's clearance, it would surely have meant disaster.

Oh, God, forbid that I should miss your instructions—to hold, or go.

Where's My Shovel?

"You want us to build an airstrip so the moon can land…?"

"You've got to be kidding. What a crazy idea. Anyone with good sense knows the moon can't land on earth!"

That's the answer Rick Speece, Wycliffe translator with the Ankave people in interior Papua New Guinea, got when he asked for help to build an airstrip so the JAARS plane could land in their valley.

Airplanes, as far as the Ankave were concerned, were like the sun and moon, always moving across the sky but never touching the earth. They had never seen an airplane sitting on the ground. They believed airplanes never came down.

But the Ankave–accepting Rick's word–built the airstrip, and their faith in Rick was not disappointed.

The airplane came down–many, many times.

Sometimes I wonder if I'd have built that airstrip.

I'm as certain as the Ankave that the moon isn't about to land on earth. I'm certain too that sophisticated, rational people don't build airstrips for the moon.

Or do they?

How far am I willing to go beyond reason and rationality to reach for the moon or, for that matter, bring it down, if that's what God wants of me?

When I read, "Faith is the assurance of the things [we] hope for, being the proof of things [we] do not see and the conviction of their reality" (Hebrews 11:1 Amplified), what is God telling me?

Lord, if you want me to build an airstrip for the moon, I'm ready–shovel in hand–to be cleared for takeoff.

Don't Be a Fool

Pilots sometimes get teased about the big watches they wear–watches with lots of buttons and so many hands it takes practice to know which one tells the time.

But the teasing ceases when it's time to know how much longer the engine will run on the gas that's left. Or the pilot is feeling for the ground on an instrument approach, counting the seconds until he expects to break out of the soup and see the end of the runway.

That's when knowing the exact time is serious business.

But I think knowing the time–numbering our days as the Psalmist says–is serious business for more than just when the fuel gauge is bumping the bottom. And it takes more than a big watch. David knew that. That's why he prayed, "Teach us to number our days and recognize how few they are; help us to spend them as we should" (Psalm 90:12 LB).

I got a birthday card recently that set me thinking about this. "Time," it reminded me, "is God's birthday gift, an earthly trust which, if invested wisely, will produce eternal treasure." The watch on my wrist never stops ticking, marking off the moments of my life–1,440 minutes each day, 10,000 each week, about 525,000 every year. It's awesome! All those minutes to spend. Wastefully? Productively? That birthday card made me wonder. Am I making the most of God's trust of time?

It's scary when you think that second by second, minute by minute, relentlessly, our days tick away. We get only one opportunity to take advantage of each second, each minute. There's no way we can live those moments over, no matter how much we wish we could. They're behind us for good or ill–forever.

"So," cautions the apostle, "be careful how you act; these are difficult days. Don't be fools; be wise; make the most of every opportunity you have for doing good" (Ephesians 5:15 LB).

Yes, Lord, teach us to number our days. Help us to spend them as we should.

Getting the Right Perspective

An airline captain friend tells the story of a flight attendant who, before departure, noticed an elderly lady sitting alone and looking extremely nervous.

Hoping to allay the woman's fears, the stewardess buckled in beside her and held her hand during takeoff. After climb-out, the "Fasten Seat Belt" sign went off, and the attendant, giving her new friend a final, comforting pat on the hand, got up to continue her work. The older lady, looking up with a cherubic smile, told the stewardess, "If you're frightened again, my dear, just come, and I'll hold your hand."

We chuckle, but how many times have we been caught when what we thought we saw or understood was not really that at all?

I'm always intrigued by those simple puzzle-page geometric drawings that flip-flop depending on how you look at them. It's a matter of perspective.

And what's perspective? The term literally suggests "looking through…seeing clearly." Obviously, it's related to the way we view something.

I find that when my perspective is right I have a much clearer view. Then it's easy to see Jesus in life's design. But too often, frequently by my own choice, my view is cloudy and dim, and I squint to see what's there.

Life is decidedly uncertain, with lots of flip-flops, and there are times when things are definitely not what they seem. But there is one perspective I never want to lose. Whether it's cloudy or clear, I know He is buckled in beside me offering the comfort of His hand in mine–not just for takeoff, but for the entire flight.

Smashed Bugs, Smashed People

I like a clean windshield.

Nothing bugs me more, whether I'm flying or driving, than bugs smashed and smeared all over the windshield.

An item in the aviation press a few years ago is still vivid in my memory. On a beautiful, clear, fall afternoon a commuter plane, letting down for landing at a midwestern city, had a call from the air traffic controller.

"You have conflicting traffic at one o'clock."

"Roger, we're looking," replied the pilot, "but we can't see too well. We've got the sun in our eyes and lots of smashed bugs on the windshield."

Those were his last words.

Moments later, both airplanes crashed to the ground, twisted pieces of wreckage.

A dozen people perished because of bugs on the windshield!

My family and friends tease me when I whip out the rags and window cleaner every time I pull up to the gas pump. Their good-natured gibes don't bother me. I want to see where I am going; I think it's important.

But not everyone agrees. I'll never forget a family trip when I was a kid. Dad stopped at a gas station in Cle Elum, Washington, where the attendant, an irascible, unkempt fellow, was not, to say it nicely, service-oriented. Churlishly he pumped the gas, but when Dad asked him to clean the bugs off the windshield, he balked.

"No use," he grumped. It'll just get dirty again," and off he stomped, leaving Dad with his mouth hanging open.

A clean windshield ranked high on my father's safety scale, and he also had an abiding passion for neatness. He grabbed a rag and cleaned it himself.

I've often thought about that little incident and chuckled over that obstinate fellow. But I believe, for all his faults, he really nailed it–clean windshields will get dirty again. What he in his stubbornness didn't want to admit was that what gets dirty needs cleaning. That's why I like my father's attitude. That's why I keep a rag and the Windex handy.

But where do I find a bottle of Windex to keep my mind and heart's vision clean and clear? Often it seems my view through the windshield of life's journey is covered with smashed bugs.

Solomon gives a frightening warning in one of his proverbs: "Where there is no vision, the people perish" (Proverbs 29:18 KJV). Smashed bugs can cause smashed lives.

So, what do we do? How do we "keep our way pure?" What can we use to clean off the smashed bugs and keep our vision polished?

I am encouraged by David, the Psalm singer, who had cleaned off his share of messy bugs.

"Have mercy on me, O God," he implored in Psalm 51. "The smashed bugs on my windshield are about to kill me…my transgressions and my sin are always before me…Cleanse me…and I will be clean" (a pilot's paraphrase).

God's mercy and our willingness for *His* washing, that's the way to keep the windshield of life clear.

On Flying Straight and Level

An aviation writer, describing the experimental Grumman X-29, says it looks as if the mechanics that built it put the wings on backwards, as though it's always flying in reverse. It goes faster that way, the engineers say, because swept-forward wings create less drag. I can understand the desire for more speed, but that isn't the X-29's only abnormality. It was designed to be unstable. For a pilot that's unbelievable.

Every pilot wants a stable airplane, whether a Piper Cub or a Boeing 747, that's designed to fly straight and level by itself. One that, even if the pilot takes his hands off the controls, and a gust of wind tips the airplane sideways, will tend to return to level flight.

Not so the X-29. But its instability wasn't a mistake. The Grumman engineers knew what they were doing when they designed the X-29 that way. They wanted an airplane that could not only go fast but could also change direction in the blink of an eye. That's how our air force pilots will someday outmaneuver the opposition and win air battles.

The engineers achieved their goal so well that not even a test pilot's consummate skill can keep the airplane under control. Any divergence from straight and level, no matter how slight, will double every 150 milliseconds–less than a blink of an eye–and before the pilot can even think about reacting, the X-29 will tumble through the sky on its way to becoming an expensive piece of junk. The engineers found the only answer to keeping the X-29 under control was to give the pilot some help. A savvy test pilot would never dare crawl into the cockpit without knowing he had a computer hooked to the controls to help him fly.

It's the computer that makes all the difference. Forty times a second it analyzes altitude and position and delicately adjusts the controls to obtain the "happy state called stability." From takeoff to landing, the pilot depends on the computer to keep him straight and level.

It seems to me that every morning when I crawl into the cockpit of the day's activities, I'd better be sure I'm plugged into the only computer that can keep me flying straight and level.

God has demonstrated time and again that He can run my life much better than I can. So, if I'm a savvy pilot, I'll ask Him to power up my inner computer–the one that promises a spirit of power, of love and of self-discipline, the one that fills me with love and joy and peace and all those other good things that make for smooth flying under good control.

PART FIVE

*On Being
a Servant*

Photo on previous page:

General Carlos P. Romulo, distinguished Filipino statesman and diplomat, here flanked by the author and Wycliffe Bible Translators founder, William Cameron Townsend, had just received on behalf of his countrymen the Helio Courier, *Spirit of Pontiac*. The airplane was given by the citizens of Pontiac, Michigan, for service among the Filipino minority language groups.

What Makes You Tick?

Almost automatically I said yes, when Major Rio Frio asked for help. It wasn't until later, when he explained his need in detail, that I had serious second thoughts.

At the time we were living in Shell Mera, an Ecuadorian frontier town nestled in the lower folds of the eastern Andes. Shell was the gateway to the jungle. From there the major had the oversight of roughly one-third of the nation—all that lay east of the Andes. Oriente Province, almost equal to the size of West Virginia, was solid jungle and, with no roads, almost totally isolated. The isolation created the major's problem.

The two of us had become good friends in the year or so my wife and I had been in Ecuador, opening up an aviation program for our Wycliffe translators. Because of our friendship, I wanted to help him if I could, but even more basic was my desire to be a servant in the name of the Lord who called me to follow His example. I wanted to make my missionary plane and pilot skills available to any and all in need. In doing so, I felt I would be showing my Savior's love.

During our deepening friendship, I hadn't been able to say much to the major about my faith. One of my missionary colleagues, a medical doctor, had attempted; but the major, holding up his hand and smiling to soften the rebuff, said, "Let's stay friends." He, like many of us, was a product of the generation that put Protestants and Catholics at odds with each other. He still tended to see those not of his particular faith as "the enemy."

But I wasn't his enemy, I was his friend, so that rancor didn't inhibit him from asking me for help. His face mirroring his concern, he grimly explained, "Don Roberto, I'm at my wit's end. I've got men starving at some of our outlying posts in the jungle. Can you fly food to them?"

His regular attempts to send food—rice and beans, flour, salt and sugar— down the rivers by dugout canoes were repeatedly frustrated, when everything went bottom up in the fierce rapids.

"My men are subsisting on whatever they can grow," he said. "Can you help me until I can work out some other means?"

I wanted to help, but his problem created one for me. I had to ask myself, *Is this what I've come to Ecuador to do—fly supplies to Ecuadorian army soldiers?* I knew some mission supporters would categorically say no. What would my donors, those who sent and supported me as a missionary, think? This didn't seem to fall within the norm of what we ordinarily expect of missionaries—or did it?

Two days later, after thinking and praying about it during many of my waking moments, I concluded it did. I decided servants don't call the shots; servants do what they are bidden, no matter how difficult or unconventional.

Three years later, after I'd flown mountains of rice, beans, flour, salt and sugar all over the eastern jungle to some mighty happy recipients, Major Rio Frio came with a second request. He was being posted to another command, and he wanted me, because I was his friend, to fly him to Quito. He had three other means of transport available, but it was with me he wanted to share his tears and deep sorrow at leaving the place, his men and the command he'd grown to love.

It was during the flight to Quito that he turned to me with a question: "Don Roberto, I'd like to know what makes you tick. I know you could stay in the U.S. and earn big money flying the airlines or doing some other work. Why do you impoverish yourself to come here to the jungle to help us?"

Fifteen minutes sufficed to tell him why: that because of what God had done for me through His Son, I was motivated to share that love. I explained how, through faith—simply believing what God told me through His Word—I accepted the gift of His Son, the Lord Jesus Christ, as my Savior. Then we looked at some verses from one of the Spanish New Testaments I always carried in the plane.

It was a very simple testimony, shouted over the roar of the engine. When I finished I looked over at the major and was surprised to see tears spilling down his cheeks. With both hands, he grabbed my arm. "Roberto, *mi amigo,* that's what I want!" There, flying among the snow-capped Andes, Major Rio Frio simply and sincerely entered into the realm of the born-again ones.

Since that time I've often reflected that it took three years and the transport of tons and tons of rice and beans and salt and flour to earn the credibility for that testimony. It reminds me of the old adage, "What you are speaks so loud I can't hear what you say." God promised to bless a servant attitude. I'm so glad I decided servants could serve soldiers.

We're cleared for takeoff–to serve.

Her First and Only Airplane Ride

When the rickety bus screeched to a stop behind the hangar, I didn't even look up. My early morning attention was totally caught up in a careful preflight inspection of the Helio Courier before starting the day's flying. It promised to be a busy day.

The crunch of shoes on gravel and a cheery greeting broke my concentration. *"Hola,* don Roberto, would it be possible for you to carry us to Arapicos?"

I glanced up, irritated with the interruption, then smiled a welcome. Miguel was a friend I had flown before. "So you want a flight to Arapicos?" I responded.

I needn't have asked. Arapicos was only 12 minutes away, and I'd been there so many times I'd almost worn a groove in the sky.

Two years earlier Miguel and his friends, along with their families, had moved across the Andes to carve farms from the isolation of eastern Ecuador's jungle. Several months earlier they had come to me begging for help. They knew my missionary plane could whisk them in minutes high over a mucky, muddy trail that on foot would normally cost them three days of agonizing slogging.

I was glad to help. That's why I was in Ecuador. I wanted to be a servant to any and all in every way I could. But I never could have guessed what this morning's offer to help would lead to.

"We'll have to hurry," I urged.

Short minutes later, after a hasty weighing and loading up, we were off and soon bouncing down at Arapicos. Again I urged Miguel to hurry as we dragged cargo to the side, out of the way. I couldn't afford to waste time on the ground.

Back in the cockpit, I jammed my seatbelt buckle home and was just settling the earphones on my head when I heard a shout. A boy had burst from the jungle at the far end of the strip. Seeing me already in the cockpit, he started running and shouting, "*Espere, espere!* (Wait, wait!)"

What was this all about? I waited while he sprinted the couple hundred yards to the plane.

"Can you carry out a load of meat?" he gasped. "They're bringing it already."

That was a normal request and no surprise. I had flown many loads of fresh meat from Arapicos, but I did wonder how they had butchered it so quickly. I didn't have long to wonder. They hadn't bothered. This meat was still on the hoof. Waddling slowly my way was a big sow—and I mean a *big* one—about to become a passenger in my airplane. Why not, they reasoned.

Live people ride the airplane, *why not* a live pig?

Jumping down from the cockpit, I waggled my finger from side to side—Latin America's universal sign for *no, absolutely, positively no!* I was prepared to be a servant, even a happy servant, but only up to a point.

"I can't carry a live pig," I explained. "Especially one that big."

And she was big. My farm-boy eye said this old sow weighed 300 pounds if she weighed an ounce.

"Then we'll kill it," they offered in chorus.

Nope. No way. I wasn't about to spend an hour pulling the floorboards and cleaning blood from the belly of my bird.

Faces fell. What to do now? They couldn't carry the meat out; it would spoil. Nor could that portly pig endure the rigors of the trail's knee-deep mud. Nope, I knew if this pig was going to market, she had to fly. And guess who was going to be the pilot on this adventure?

"OK," I agreed, letting my heart take over from my head.

"Get some vine from the jungle. Hurry, let's tie her up tight, and I'll fly her out alive."

But that sow had a thing about flying. Right up front, she let everyone know she didn't want any part of such foolishness. Furthermore, she didn't want her legs tied, and she told the whole world about it.

But who cares what pigs do or don't like? The fellows bound her legs like Houdini, grabbed all the handles available, ears, tail and legs, and unceremoniously dumped her in, where I tied her down as best I could. Then, belted in again and earphones on, I could hardly hear the answer to my "ready for takeoff" call. The whole airplane was reverberating with that pig's squeals. Even the bellowing engine on takeoff couldn't drown her protests.

But leveling off in cruise, I suddenly realized she must be overcome with the joys of flight; no more squeals. *Good,* I thought. *She's going to enjoy her first and only airplane ride.*

Then, glancing back to see how she was doing, I looked her right in the eye. Feet loose and standing with legs splayed out for balance, she was quietly oinking her contentment, the picture of a happy pig.

Lord, I breathed, don't let her try for the copilot's job. Just keep her happy and quiet until I can get this airplane on the ground.

He did. She did. And I did. And I'll tell you, this pilot was never happier to discharge a passenger. It doesn't take much to make me a happy servant.

Right out of the Book

Would you believe JAARS was cleared for takeoff in A.D. 33, give or take a little?

No? Well, I can't say that I blame you. We all know the only fliers in those days were the birds. Aluminum and airfoils were still two millennia down the road.

A doctor gives us the account in chapter six of Acts. The disciples were in a stew—quite literally. Problems in the kitchen and dining room were getting them down. Dr. Luke doesn't tell us if it was big, blustery Peter or not, but one of the twelve finally called a meeting and vented his frustrations. He said, "We mustn't neglect preaching for waiting on tables. Now look around…and select seven men; and we will put them in charge of this business" (Acts 6:2-3 LB).

But, you are wondering, *what has this to do with JAARS?* A lot. In principle, specialized Christian service was born in A.D. 33. Peter set forth the philosophy: Get Bible translators out of the "kitchen." They shouldn't neglect translation to administer an airline.

So Wycliffe selected "men of good reputation, full of the Spirit and of wisdom, well thought of by everyone, and put them in charge of the task." That's how JAARS was born. Today many Stephens and Philips are scattered across the globe, involved in aviation, construction and maintenance, information technology, purchasing and shipping, trucking, vernacular media and much more. Some fly, some fix and some fetch.

And the results? Exactly the same now as in A.D. 33. "The Word of God spread. The number of disciples…increased rapidly and a large number…became obedient to the faith" (Acts 6:7 NIV).

Thank God He cleared us for takeoff.

Why Do We Do It?

Dr. David Smith thinks our JAARS mission pilots are incredible.

Dave, an ophthalmologist who thinks nothing of sewing a new cornea into a living eye with stitches so tiny he has to use a microscope to see what he is doing, stands in awe of "pioneer missionaries and fearless jungle pilots."

Not long ago he visited Ecuador to see Wycliffe in action. He especially wanted to learn what was happening among the Waorani (formerly called Auca and known for their savage killing of five missionaries in 1956). Dave vividly remembered the stories of those bloody scenes on Palm Beach. He'd heard that the gospel had changed those killers into preachers. He wanted to see for himself.

Later, he said that it's one thing to hear the stories in your living room and quite another to climb into a JAARS plane and fly across the jungle for a visit. He wrote me his impressions:

> I don't know if I can convey what it was like. We were flying over the dense Amazon jungle in a small, single-engine JAARS Helio Courier, when clouds suddenly enveloped the airplane so thickly that nothing was visible outside the cockpit. Only the drone of the engine broke the loud silence.
>
> Suddenly I was completely disoriented. Were we right side up, turning, or upside down? No way could I tell. I wanted to take the keys from my pocket and let them dangle, to see which way was up. I felt like pulling my feet up, because I knew those trees were getting closer and closer as we descended.
>
> I was scared. I had thought I knew what made missionaries tick. Now I wondered. What kind of man will fly an airplane in a place like this every day? Exposed to malaria, amoeba, tropical disease and danger as a daily way of life–why does he do it?

Great wealth? Hardly. He lives on whatever friends like us and churches send him each month, with never enough for savings.

Great esteem? He is isolated in his jungle outpost from all except those who have made the same commitment. Why, then, does he do it?

When I stepped out on the blood-bought soil of that short, grassy airstrip chopped from the jungle by the Waoranis, I knew.

As I looked into their smiling faces, I knew.

When I took their hands and heard their warm "Buenos días," I knew.

That night, lying snug in my bed back at Limoncocha, the events of the day flashed vividly through my mind. I could hardly believe, that very day, my hand had held the hand of one of the killers. Kimo had slain a missionary. Now he was following Jesus and preaching to his people. He had baptized the slain missionary's son on the same jungle beach where he had killed his father.

> His hand I held but a moment;
> His smile somewhat longer was there.
> His heart met with mine for an hour,
> But forever our Jesus we'll share.

That's right, Dave. That's why we do it.

I've Been Promoted

Bill Cristobal was flying home after carrying a Wycliffe translation team to Papua New Guinea's western highlands. Low on fuel, he had to land at the highland town of Mt. Hagen.

On approach he couldn't believe his eyes. There, sitting on the ramp, was the very same immense, heavy-lift Boeing 107, twin-engine helicopter he'd flown years ago in Alaska before coming to fly with JAARS. What was it doing here in Papua New Guinea? Jumping out of his helicopter, he wasted no time getting over to see the "ol' bird, N6675D."

There he had a second surprise. Two of the crew were buddies he used to work with. Amid backslaps and handshakes, they urged Bill to climb aboard for a few minutes. "Come on. See all the fancy new radios we have now."

Memories flooded back as Bill settled himself into the cockpit. He remembered the great satisfaction he had experienced when 3,000 horsepower strained at his command, lifting huge logs from steep mountainsides or setting high-tension-line towers in the wilderness.

His gaze wandered around the cockpit. After nine years of flying his little JAARS three-seater, he'd forgotten how cavernous this helicopter was! *It would be fun to fly this again,* he thought, as his hands fell to the controls with practiced ease.

A twinge of envy hit him. Suddenly he wondered, *had he been left behind in the aviation world? Was he missing something out here flying Bible translators in the backwaters of civilization?*

Glancing up, his eye caught sight of his sturdy little blue and white helicopter across the ramp. That dependable machine had just delivered a

Bill Cristobal in his "beautiful machine."

translation team—and the opportunity for a whole nation of people, men and women, boys and girls, to have God's Word.

You know, thought Bill, *I've been promoted—promoted to serve people—and more than just their physical needs, their spiritual needs too.*

After goodbyes and handshakes all around, Bill walked back across the ramp and settled contentedly into his own cockpit. Reaching up, he gave the chopper an affectionate pat. "You're a beautiful machine, doing a superb job. I'm glad we can do it together."

Thanks for reminding us, Bill. Lasting satisfaction doesn't come from what we have, but from what we can do with it.

Christians Are Not Perfect, Just Forgiven

There are times I've wished life were a tape recorder that I could reverse, erase the tape and start afresh. I still shudder with memories of episodes I wish I could re-record.

I'll never forget one that occurred when my family and I were part of the JAARS team in the Philippines.

My task that day was a routine flight to pick up a translation team coming out of their remote village to participate in a four-week-long linguistic workshop. The day turned out to be anything but routine.

First, the weather was poor–low clouds, wind and occasional showers. The destination was miles away. There were no weather reports between home and destination, and no radio navigation aids. All this started the adrenaline count soaring upward.

Then it shot up another two counts on the approach to landing. The translators' airstrip was a miniscule slash in the trees at the far end of a narrow, deep valley. Once you've plunged into the valley's throat, you're committed to land–somewhere. It's too narrow to turn in, and the surrounding mountains are too high to climb over.

This time it was worse. Violent wind grabbed me in its teeth and shook the airplane, pitching me up and pushing me down. I fought the controls to keep the wings out of the clutching trees on either side. That wasn't all. At the approach end of the strip stood a spirit tree, an immense barrier that could not be chopped down because people in the area believed that "the spirits live in it." On every landing I feared my left wing would slice through that tree. This day I wondered if the whole airplane might be impaled.

But I made it, pent-up breath exploding with relief as I smacked the Helio down right on the end of the strip. But relief turned to fright again when the plane began to slide on the wet, grease-slick grass, right up to prop-chopping distance from the trees at the other end. When I finally got turned around and taxied back to stop in front of the translators' house, my mouth was so dry I couldn't spit. But I wasn't through with problems yet! There, waiting for me was a mountain of cargo stacked beside the airstrip.

Good grief, I thought. *They're going out for only four weeks.* That pile looked like a year's worth at least. I was certain it was far more than I could carry in one flight. I groaned. I didn't want to make another trip in here today. The turbulence was enough to eat you alive.

But after carefully weighing everything, I found I could make all that cargo fit, *if* we left one item behind, a three-gallon pail of rice with cans of sardines buried in it. We were overweight by the exact amount of that bucket of rice.

Since there was lots of rice where we were going, the solution was obvious. "We'll leave it behind." But my suggestion fell on deaf ears. That bucket of rice had to go. I said no. They said yes. I said no again. They insisted. My adrenaline count, still high, started going higher.

I offered to buy a bag of rice and a whole carton of sardines when we got back to the translation center. No way. It was not debatable. They had to have *that* bucket of rice.

I wish I could say my good sense and loving servant heart finally took charge, but it wasn't so. That hairy approach and landing still churned in my mind. I had no desire to repeat it. The takeoff and departure through that wind-tunnel valley would be no picnic. The only way to meet the translators' wishes would be to divide the load in half and make two shuttle flights to another, longer strip nearby. Shuttle flights meant I'd have to attend that picnic twice. It also threw all my careful fuel planning into a cocked hat. I didn't want to do it.

Safety was not the issue. I knew the departure wouldn't be life threatening, just scary. Had it been—and the translators knew this—there would have been no debate. At issue was an uptight pilot with his dander up, who didn't have the grace to back down. I've squirmed with the pain of that memory many times in the years since.

Long ago I agreed with God that His orders were my command. I really wanted to do to others what I would have them do to me (Matthew 7:12 NIV). I really wanted to show love by my actions and be a willing servant. Now I'd blown it.

But thank God, He forgives, as did my colleagues. I can't back up the tape and erase that folly, but He can and did. I'm a prime example of the bumper sticker wisdom I saw recently: "Christians aren't perfect, just forgiven."

And wouldn't you know, though I hate to admit it, the second approach and landing was a piece of cake.

Cleared for takeoff and still learning.

Move Over, Doug!

I received a letter the other day from Doug Deming, a longtime JAARS pilot in Peru. Doug had come to the JAARS center, and we'd been talking about…well, I'll let Doug tell you.

Bob,

Remember you and I were talking about the problems we all experience in being a servant? It reminds me of the couplet, "It takes more grace than I can tell, to play the second fiddle well." And that reminds me of Barnabas in the book of Acts.

This all came to mind the other day when Dave Ramsdale buckled into the left seat of the twin Evangel, and I walked around to the right. I must confess that after all these years it's still hard for me to give up the captain's seat and give another pilot control. Now I have to. My assigned task is to push good men up the ladder. It's my primary job. Training. Teaching. Motivating men to excellence.

Training takes long hours of discussing the intricacies of flying, and long hard hours of pressuring the student till he sweats. He has to know the right lever to push or pull when an engine sighs and dies. If he doesn't, he and his passenger might not survive.

I was proud of Dave. He did a good job no matter what emergency situation I set up. Glancing across the throttle quadrant at him perspiring in the left seat, I began to identify with Barnabas. Barnabas moved over and served in the right seat, so Paul could begin learning the captain's duties. And Paul, like Dave and the other men I work with, was dedicated and sharp, a quick learner and a leader.

They made a good missionary team, Barnabas and Paul, and Barnabas did his training job well. In fact, so well that soon Scripture notes a switch from Barnabas and Paul to Paul and Barnabas. Paul had taken command. Barnabas had moved to the right seat and helped a good man become better.

But Barnabas, ever the sensitive trainer, didn't stop there. Another man on the crew needed help: young, impetuous John Mark. In frustration he had thrown in the towel and gone home. Barnabas, over Captain Paul's objection, sought him out, took him under his wing, discipled him and produced another winner. It was Mark who wrote the Gospel easiest to translate into other languages because of its clear narrative style. Score one more for Barnabas.

God doesn't ordain us all to be captains all the time. Some of us have quiet, behind-the-scenes responsibilities. I don't really mind moving to the right seat, especially when I remember it was our Teacher, the ultimate Servant, who took a towel and washed feet, and finally went all the way to a cross.

Your servant trainer,

Doug

Just Useful Talents

By anybody's standards Walt Agee was a success. Everybody was sure of it, but him.

In Walt's own words he's "an inventive, fix-it type. I like working with my hands," he says. "Give me anything mechanical, and I'll make it work." True, and Walt knew it. But a few years ago, in his low moments, he wondered, *How really useful am I in God's kingdom?*

Discouragement plagued him even more when he'd hear preachers talk about spiritual gifts. Walt wasn't sure that his abilities–to run a print shop; typeset the New Testament in a hundred different languages (using the incredibly precise type-fonts he'd made); or use a camera he had built– were really spiritual gifts. Even some of his pastoral counselors encouraged him to look for "other *genuine* gifts of the Spirit."

He laments, "I was told mine were just useful talents." His self-esteem plunged so low he had to look up to see bottom!

Then he happened on a conversation the Lord had with Moses, recorded in Exodus 31. The Lord was commissioning some special help for Moses to build the tabernacle and...

"See," the Lord told Moses, "I have chosen Bezalel...and I have filled him with the Spirit of God, with skill, ability and knowledge in all kinds of crafts, to make artistic designs for work in gold, silver and bronze, to cut and set stones, to work in wood and to engage in all kinds of craftsmanship" (Exodus 31:2-5 NIV).

Walt let those words sink in: skill, ability and knowledge, filled with the Spirit of God. He suddenly saw those fonts, those typeset pages of Scripture, those machines he kept in repair, as a vital part of the building of God's house–and himself as a skilled craftsman endowed with excellent and genuine gifts.

He has never wondered again.

The Big Father's Work

Recently a thrilling letter came to JAARS. A check fluttered from it, but that wasn't the best part. The real thrill came when we realized the letter and the gift came from people living along the swampy Sepik River in Papua New Guinea. Fifteen years earlier, some of these people had never even seen a check or held a pencil. Now a thriving, excited congregation, they asked their pastor Joel Kapawi to write to JAARS. They wanted to help with a memorial to Uncle Cam. Here's Joel's letter to us—and to you:

> To all my brothers and sisters, in the name of Jesus Christ
> I write this letter to you.
>
> We Christian men and women of Hauna want to help you with the very big house [Townsend Memorial Building] to help us think back in remembrance of this man Uncle Cam. For many years you people have helped us. We know this man, Uncle Cam, got this work going, but now he has died. Therefore, this is the work you, and us too, are doing now. Why? Because many areas of many countries have not yet received the Bible Book in their language.
>
> This work of ours must go ahead. We must not be lazy or rest, but we must work hard this work, which Uncle Cam started. So we have put this little bit of money in this letter. God has blessed our church at Hauna, and therefore we want to help you with this little bit.
>
> That is all. This little bit of talk of ours is finished. You must stand up strong and tighten your bones. Now go ahead with the Big Father's work.

And in that letter was a gift of $100! That's the Bible translation team in action! Neat to be a part of all that, isn't it? To finish the Big Father's work.

Wanted: Finishers

These days the bookstores and magazine racks are filled with motivational writing. There is no lack of authors with ideas on how to get started.

That's good. Insightful advice is something we all can use, because sparking initiative, setting goals and developing a game plan are often difficult tasks.

But, on the other side of the coin, I don't see much written on finishing. Not many speak up for sticking with something until it's done, for hanging in there when the early excitement fades and perseverance becomes a matter of discipline and guts. Not many speak up for finishing the course.

The book *Voyager* could be a how-to manual on that subject. It is the story of the perseverance of two pilots who, with "almost superhuman physical and psychological effort," finished the course. Jeana Yeager and Dick Rutan circled the world nonstop without refueling, something that had never been done before. In the process they conquered what is probably the last first in aviation.

You probably remember the flight. The TV news kept us informed morning, noon and night during the nine days they bounced around the edges of typhoons and battled mechanical problems, to finally achieve something that often seemed beyond reach or reasonable expectation.

Success didn't come easily. The plaudits that came their way were hard-earned. Yeager and Rutan, and Rutan's brother Burt (who designed the frail-appearing, stranger-looking *Voyager*), along with a small cadre of friends, struggled through six years of vexing setbacks. Successes were so infrequent they despaired of ever achieving their goal.

Technical problems gave trouble enough, said Yeager, but those you could work out, fix and tweak. Human factor problems proved the most difficult; the stickiest were created by strong personalities under stress grating on one another. Ultimately, two people were expected to live and work for 11 or 12 days crammed into a cockpit the size of a telephone booth laid on its side. Could the teamwork essential to success be retained when already it was beginning to unravel? About midpoint in the six-year project, Jeana Yeager said she was fed up. "I would have left if I could, but I couldn't. I had made a commitment. I had never stopped short of finishing anything before, and I wasn't about to now."

Good for you, Jeana! I wish we all had that attitude. It seems our generation is perilously near the "I'm fed up, so I'm going to quit" mentality. We're often ready to give up before we fairly get started. It matters little whether it's marriage, the job, problems at school, church or whatever.

What strikes me is that Yeager and Rutan willingly endured their six years of travail for a "corruptible crown." Oh, it was a nice one—the prestigious Presidential Citizens Medal, one of the highest awards our government can give a civilian. And the airplane is displayed in the Smithsonian's National Air and Space Museum alongside the *Wright Flyer* and *The Spirit of St Louis*. That's good. They earned it. Any of us would have reason to be proud of such accolades. But one day those medals will rust and the ribbons decay. Their lovely reward will be a pile of dust.

How about us who work for a crown that is incorruptible? Are we willing to keep going, even when it is a struggle? Are we willing to work as hard as the *Voyager* crew, but for the eternal reward that's promised to those who finish the course?

We need Paul's reminder: "Let us not get tired of doing what is right, for after a while we will reap a harvest of blessing if we don't get discouraged and give up" (Galatians 6:9 LB).

And another: "You need to persevere so that when you have done the will of God, you will receive what he has promised" (Hebrews 10:36 NIV).

Let's hear it for the finishers!

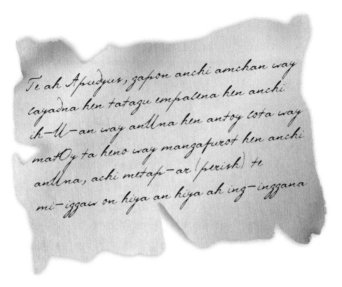

Garbage Wasn't the Word

I'll never forget the time in the Philippines when Joanne Shetler was searching for a special word. She wanted the right way to express *perish* in Balangao, the language of a tribe of former headhunters in the northern mountains of Luzon. She'd been looking for weeks, but she couldn't find the right word.

It boggles my mind when I watch our Wycliffe translators unravel an unwritten language, first by listening to it, then by putting it on paper and eventually by translating God's Word. It is a difficult and demanding job.

I've always thought that, by comparison, flying my mission plane in the jungles and mountains was the easy end of the Bible translation task, even though it is an important and rewarding one. For example, with the airplane we turned five days of difficult and dangerous overland travel into a 21-minute flight for Jo and her translation partner, Anne. Living among the Balangao people would have been much more complicated, if not impossible, without air service.

In the years I've been serving Wycliffe Bible Translators, I've learned that the first thing a translator wants to do after getting an adequate grasp of the language is translate some Bible verses. Like many, Jo wanted her first effort at translation to be a clear declaration of God's love for the Balangao people. She chose John 3:16.

Word by word she began rendering it in the language: "For God so loved the world that he gave his one and only son that whoever believes in him shall not…." She had to stop there–stymied. She couldn't find a Balangao word that meant *perish*.

For weeks she asked questions using all the techniques she had been taught. Finally a word surfaced–*basura,* which is Spanish for *garbage.* How that word made its way to the mountains to become part of the Balangao vocabulary, no one knows. But certainly *garbage* is not what God's Holy Spirit intended to convey by the word *perish,* as we find it in John 3:16.

One day, some weeks later, Jo had worked through the morning hours with Tekla, a young mother who, when she learned that the translators' goal was to give the Balangaos the words of God in their language, wanted to help. She dedicated as much time from her busy days as she could.

It was noontime, and Tekla declared she would go home to cook food for her family. "Juami, you come and eat with us," she said, using their name for Jo.

"OK, you go get the rice pot on. I'll be there in a few minutes." Jo was glad for the invitation, since she was alone in the village at the time. A little later she climbed Tekla's notched-pole front steps, opened the front door, and scooped up Tekla's little two-year-old, Anna. The toddler, always glad to see her Aunt Juami, squealed with delight as Jo loved her up. Then Jo, alternately hugging Anna and then swinging her in her arms, stepped toward the door. "I'm just going to throw you away."

Another squeeze, more giggles, and Jo again swung her toward the door. "I'm going to throw you away."

Tekla, busy at the fire table, looked up in alarm and, throwing up her hand, interrupted Anna's excited squeals. "Juami, don't say that. Oh Juami, don't say that."

Chagrined, Jo pulled up short. "What did I say? Did I say something wrong?"

"No, Juami, it's just that you used our word *metapar.* We use that only for something that is gone forever, something we'll never get back."

Jo bolted down her rice. She couldn't wait to return to the translation desk and the completion of John 3:16. And Tekla? It wasn't long before she

On Being a Servant

became the first Balangao to put her trust in the One who could keep her safe forever, the One who would never let her perish. With that same trust, we're cleared for takeoff–never to perish.

*Te ah Apudyus, gapon anchi amchan way layadna hen tatagu empalena hen anchi ih-à-an way anàna hen antoy lota way matéy ta heno way mangafurot hen anchi anàna, achi **metap-ar** (perish) te mi-iggaw on hiya an hiya ah ing-inggana* (John 3:16 in the Balangao language).

Cleared for Landing

It's funny how you remember certain things and forget others.

Even though it happened 50 years ago I'll never forget my first landing on a primitive "jungle airstrip." It's still as fresh in my memory as the day I was first pushed out of the nest to fly solo in the little yellow Piper Cub.

It was early 1956. A couple of months earlier I had delivered JAARS' first Helio Courier from the Kansas factory to Ecuador. Now, I wanted to put it to work. Several of the translation teams were already busy whacking out airstrips–really short airstrips. Their eager ears had soaked up all the hype about the Helio's fantastic ability for short take-offs and landings. The company wasn't exaggerating. It really did. And certainly the advertised, tongue-in-cheek, "tennis court" was easier to cut from virgin forest than the longer strips everyone was accustomed to.

Glen Turner's was the first of such airstrips. Glen and his wife, Jean, had agreed to begin their linguistic efforts among the Jívaro (now called Shuar), a group of people who had been widely feared as killers–killers with a specialty. The original "shrinks," their reputation was gained from the practice of shrinking their enemies' severed heads to the size of a doubled-up fist. Now, however, they had peacefully invited the Turners to live among them. And Glen was eager to put hiking muddy, mucky jungle trails behind him.

I knew the strip would be as good as Glen and the Shuar men could make it, but they faced a Herculean job, whittling an airstrip, even a short one, from virgin rain forest. They had key help from fellow Wycliffe member, Don Johnson. Don, a lumberman's son from Washington State, had slogged in with his monstrous old chain saw and woodsman's knowledge to help wrest that 400-foot airstrip from the tangle of giant trees.

I was wary when Glen radioed that his new airstrip was ready. I knew he had cleared the requested 400-foot length, but two days of heavy thunderstorms earlier in the week made me extra cautious.

"But Glen, are you sure it is firm enough?" I quizzed. Nowadays, due to more stringent government regulations, JAARS often requires pilots to make a ground inspection, but in those early days we were at the beginning of the learning curve.

Glen replied, "I've been out walking it, jumping up and down on it and I really think it is solid enough for you to land on. We've had two days of sun out here to help dry it out."

"Well, OK," I said. "I'll come out this afternoon and have a look."

It was only a 23-minute flight. I calculated I could quickly fly out, do an inauguration landing and easily be back in an hour and a half. But just thinking about it gave a jump-start to the butterflies in my stomach.

I circled around for a good look. *Wow!* I thought, *Am I expected to land this airplane in that miniscule machete slash?* The more I looked, the shorter it got. *I better do this quickly or it'll vanish.*

There was one thing in its favor: The approach end was clear; a 20-foot bluff fell away to the Chinimbi River. It was the opposite end that gave me pause—a solid, green wall of trees, 200 feet tall—and only 400 feet away.

I sent a quick arrow-prayer heavenward. *Please Lord, help me to not mess up this brand new airplane.* Landing safely on this nail-biter was quite an order for this new-to-the-jungle pilot. The airplane was designed to do it, with its short takeoff and landing capability, but was the pilot as capable? *Well, we'll see!* I thought, as I took a deep breath and circled for the approach. There has to be a first time for everything.

I had learned from day one of my flight training that good landings began with a good approach. Get that right and spot landings were simple. Well...almost.

The trick is to look at the spot where you want to land. Don't concentrate on that green wall of trees at the far end. Do that and you'll most surely hit it. So I refused to look, but believe me, I knew it was there—a surer stop than any Navy carrier's arresting gear.

I needn't have worried. Practice paid off, and I touched down exactly where I aimed, about 50 feet from the edge of the bluff. And there I stopped—right there. Talk about short landings! That airplane didn't roll 50 feet. It couldn't, not with the wheels buried to the hubs in mud. The abrupt stop threw the tail up, forcing the spinning prop into the ground and throwing mud all over the top of the left wing. When the tail banged back down I let out a whoosh of pent-up breath. I was down and apparently all in one piece.

On Being a Servant

Killing the idling engine, I jumped out to survey the situation. My major concern was the prop. Propellers are designed to slice air, not airstrips, and this one didn't adapt well to its role as a shovel. Nearly three inches of each tip was curled back on itself.

"Hey, Glen," I shouted, "We'll need some tools. Have you got a hammer and an axe?"

"Sure," he said, wondering, I suppose, what this disgusted pilot was planning to chop off. No way could he imagine fixing bent propeller blades with a hammer and an axe.

"It should be easy," I told him, wishing I had as much confidence as I wanted him to think I had. Using the flat side of the axe as an anvil, I carefully used the hammer to beat those prop tips back where they had been before this unfortunate event. To check my work, I ran the engine up. Smooth, with no vibrations. *OK,* I thought. *Half the job is done. Now, how do I get this airplane out of the mud? Further work on the prop will have to wait until I get back to Shell Mera.*

There is nothing more helpless than an airplane stuck in the mud. But we had lots of eager Shuar helpers, and Glen explained in their explosively staccato language what we needed to do—dig. They fell to, and the mud flew. It wasn't long before my poor bird was out of the muck, on solid ground, and only about 75 feet from where I touched down. Had I only known! But this was not the time for 20/20 hindsight. It wasn't long until we had the Helio positioned with its tail tucked up to the green wall for departure. The takeoff was anticlimactic. I was off and away, happy to leave the mud behind.

Now, many years later, and after uncounted landings in that machete slash, the New Testament is complete, pastors are trained, churches are established and Shuar people are busy translating an abridged Old Testament. They even have their own radio station. And now, best of all, they don't take heads; they seek lost souls.

And how about me? One thing I know for sure, that after more than 50 years of flying and multiplied thousands of flight hours, it's my time to turn the aviating over to others. As an earlier servant put it, "This is my assigned moment for others to move into the center while I slip off to the sidelines" (John 3:30, The Message).

It's time for me to give the keys to a younger pilot. Like me, he or she will be technically competent, and spiritually motivated to share

Christ and His Word through their lives and technical work. The pilot may be from another country or different color, but he or she will climb in, buckle the seat belt and, with youthful enthusiasm, listen for their "Cleared for Takeoff."

Then, one day, perhaps sooner, perhaps later, I'll hear my final clearance with the Controller's loving words echoing in my earphones, "You are cleared to land, my good and faithful servant. Welcome home."

The author with his family, December 1959 on their departure from Wycliffe's jungle linguistic/translation center, Limón Cocha (Lemon Lake), Ecuador, for the Philippines. From the left: Louise, holding baby Deborah, Kathleen, Rebecca and Ruth. The Griffins' jungle-style house is visible in the left background.

The author invites you to climb aboard. Let's go flying!

Missions
Update

Photo on previous page:

The Quest built Kodiak turboprop was specifically conceived by aircraft designer Tom Hamilton to meet the needs of missionary bush pilots serving in geographically-challenged areas where rugged reliability and excellent performance characteristics are especially critical. The turbine engine uses widely available and less costly jet fuel. The Kodiak will be a valued part of the JAARS fleet of the future. Photo by Quest Aircraft Company, 2006.

Reflections

Wycliffe Bible Translators has set before itself an exciting goal: to see a translation project underway in every language needing one, by the year 2025. We call it Vision 2025.

It's a daunting task. Some 2,600 indigenous language groups still wait. That translates to countless millions of people who don't have the Gospel in the language of their hearts.

JAARS is eagerly seeking to help make Vision 2025 a reality, to speed Bible translation for all people. For many years JAARS was known as the "Jungle Aviation And Radio Service." Throughout its history, *service* has been—and still is—the operative JAARS word. That hasn't changed in the past 50 years.

However, certain aspects of the program are changing. Notable already are the color and nationalities of the staff. Personnel, both men and women, now come from around the globe. They are not only pilots, mechanics and radio technicians, but also machinists, information technologists, builders and more than a hundred other vocations, each one "filled with the Spirit of God, with skill, ability and knowledge in all kinds of crafts…" (Exodus 31:2-5). And each is imbued with the same driving vision—to be the best possible servant in the ministry of Bible translation to the glory of God.

Another significant change is the addition of turbine-engine-powered aircraft to the JAARS fleet. A worldwide scarcity of aviation gasoline is giving impetus to the use of turboprop aircraft that use jet fuel, easily available everywhere.

The new Kodiak, carefully designed with missionary needs uppermost in mind, will soon be in service. This new airplane will, in some instances, replace the Helio Courier, JAARS' workhorse for 50 years. By necessity the STOL (short takeoff and landing) airplanes will, in many locations, continue to rule the roost. The Kodiak will meet that need and JAARS expects, Lord willing, to put at least 10 of them into service in the next few years.

Already two Pilatus Porter PC-6 turbine-powered aircraft are serving in Southeast Asia and soon, Lord willing, the larger Pilatus PC-12 will join them. The PC-12 has the range, short-field capability and speed to enable medical emergency flights and evacuations, as well as carry out normal missions supporting Bible translation.

Helicopters will continue to find their necessary niche where the terrain is so steep and rough that building airstrips is impossible.

And then, speaking of change, space will not permit to tell of the rapid advances in today's computer technology and its use in the translation ministry. Incredible, almost instant, worldwide communications via email and telephone, newly developed software with programs to speed the task, often doubling the effectiveness of the translator, are just a few of the cutting edge advances being developed by JAARS' information technologists. It's virtually mind boggling.

That's what JAARS is all about. Technology and translation. Missionary aircraft and computers made effective by humble servants. Bibleless people and a great vision.

Decades ago, Uncle Cam Townsend urged us:

> Dear ones,
>
> By love serve one another.
>
> Finish the task.
>
> Translate the Scriptures into every language.

Now I add my challenge to his: Let's do it!
You have the keys. You are cleared for take-off.

The Swiss-built Pilatus PC-6 "Turbo Porter" is not new to JAARS. One was flown in Nepal in the 1970s when aviation gasoline became unavailable. Now the need exists again for the same reason, this time in Southeast Asia. The Porter is a versatile high performance STOL-type aircraft. Photos by Gerry Gardner.

Termed a "Versatile Freighter" by the builder, the Pilatus PC-12 is a high performance turbine powered airplane carrying nine passengers plus two crew with a payload of 2,500 pounds at a cruise speed of over 250 kts. The aircraft's ability to operate out of relatively short, unimproved runways combined with excellent speed and range will make it a useful tool in southeast Asia. Photo by Gerry Gardner.

Have you been touched by these true stories from the pages of recent history? The next pages in the saga could be yours. Would you like to see more lives changed by the Word of God? You can support the work of Bible translation through your prayers and gifts. You can join the team striving to make Vision 2025 a reality.

To learn how:
Call toll free: 1-800-890-0628
Visit the JAARS website: www.jaars.org
Write to:
    JAARS Inc.
    PO Box 248
    Waxhaw, NC 28173

Thank you for your commitment to help speed the Bible translation task.

Available from
Harvest Day Books

Power of God's Word/Inspiring Stories

Together We Can!
A Mosaic of Stories and Devotions Displaying the Impact of God's Word
By Aretta Loving

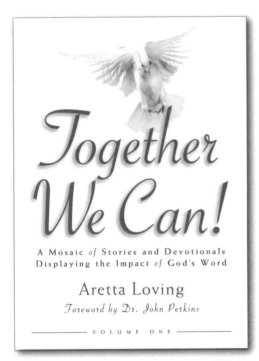

$12.95

"Together We Can! brings us stories about the truth of God's Word, changed lives, miracles, and increased faith. The one thing they all have in common is the power of the Word of God ..."
—Dr. John R. Watters,
Exec. Dir. Wycliffe International

William Cameron Townsend, my late husband, founded Wycliffe Bible Translators. If he were alive today, he would heartily endorse Together We Can! The stories display his philosophy: working together with others—and his attitude and life motto: serving others in love. As you read this book, you'll be encouraged and challenged to work with and serve others.
—Elaine Townsend

Harvest
Day
Books

Order at www.ReadingUp.com

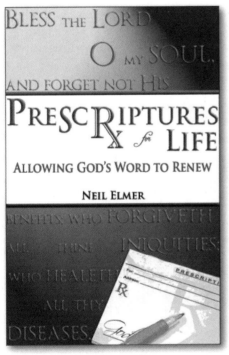

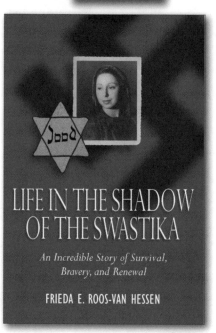

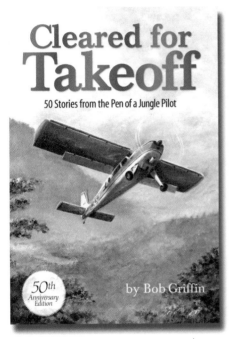

Order Form

For additional copies of *Cleared For Takeoff* or any other title from Harvest Day Books, please complete the following information or visit the publisher's web site:

www.ReadingUp.com

Discounts are available for bulk orders and to bookstores, libraries, and other retailers.

Fax orders:	(231)929-1993
Telephone orders:	(231)929-1999
E-mail orders:	Orders@BookMarketingSolutions.com
Postal orders:	BMS
	10300 E. Leelanau Court
	Traverse City, MI 49684

~~~~~~

Please send _____ **copies of** *Cleared For Takeoff* $12.95
Please send _____ **copies of** *Together We Can!* $12.95
Please send _____ **copies of** *Jungle Jewels & Jaguars* $15.95
Please send _____ **copies of** *Prescriptures for Life* $15.95
Please send _____ **copies of** *Life in the Shadow of the Swastika* $15.95

I understand that I may return any of them for a full refund–for any reason, no questions asked.

Name:_____

Address: _____

City: _____ State: _____ Zip: _____

E-mail address: _____

Phone (in case we need to contact you) _____

Sales Tax: Please add 6% for products being shipped to Michigan addresses.

Shipping by air:
US: $4.50 for the first book and $0.50 for each additional book.
International: $9.00 for the first book and $5.00 for each additional book (estimate).

TOTAL $ _____

Payment:	Check	Money Order		
Credit Card:	Visa	MasterCard	Discover	AmEx

Card Number: _____

Name on Card: _____ Exp. Date: _____/_____